COUNTRY PINE FURNITURE

COUNTRY PINE FURNITURE

CONSTANCE KING

CHARTWELL
BOOKS, INC.

A QUINTET BOOK

Published by Chartwell Books
A Division of Book Sales, Inc.
110 Enterprise Avenue
Secaucus, New Jersey 07094

ISBN 1-55521-405-3

This book was designed and produced by
Quintet Publishing Limited
6 Blundell Street
London N7 9BH

Creative Director: Peter Bridgewater
Art Director: Ian Hunt
Designer: Annie Moss
Project Editor: Judith Simons
Editors: Patricia Bayer, Henrietta Wilkinson
Picture Researcher: Liz Eddison

Typeset in Great Britain by
Central Southern Typesetters, Eastbourne
Manufactured in Hong Kong by Regent Publishing
Services Limited
Printed in Hong Kong by Leefung-Asco Printers Limited

CONTENTS

INTRODUCTION

PINE FURNITURE holds the lead in contemporary interiors as it blends well with the primitive paintings, folk textiles and richly patterned ceramic tiles that are now so fashionable. At the same time, the warm colour of the wood looks effective in the most advanced modern settings, resulting in its use as a foil for stark, abstract paintings and progressive metal-framed furniture. Originally considered a wood that was mainly suitable for utilitarian areas of the house, pine is now accepted in the most elegant surroundings and can look as good in a Munich drawing room as a Boston kitchen. Antique and modern pine can be used together to good effect, and as the wood blends so happily with others, it is extremely versatile and as likely to be found in town as in the country.

Most of the pine furniture that is offered for sale in antiques shops has been stripped and waxed, and, consequently, old and reproduction pieces do not differ as greatly in effect as the sophisticated, highly polished items in walnut or mahogany. This gives the interior decorator a great advantage, since the variety of furniture on offer is so great that there are few areas of the home, no matter how small or awkwardly shaped, that cannot be enhanced by a chest, corner cupboard or even sleigh bed of this wood.

A number of modern craftsmen specialize in the construction of well-made, and therefore expensive, work that is frequently far superior to that of the past. The Victorian country carpenter considered pine furniture the most economical of his products, to be concealed with coats of paint or stain. Today it is appreciated for its individual merit, and the colour and grain are lovingly revealed.

The acceptance of pine as a wood that is beautiful in its own right became general in the 1960s. Scandinavian designers had revived interest in lighter woods, and their influence on contemporary taste was so great that craftsmen in many other countries began to construct furniture that showed the grain and tone of the wood to advantage. No longer smothered with paint, it was left in its natural state so that its full potential was revealed.

Antiques dealers and interior decorators looked again at neglected kitchen dressers, blanket chests and panelled cupboards, and removed layers of old paint to expose the original constructions. Carried away with enthusiasm, they treated everything from cheap bedroom suites to elegant marbled pedestals, thereby ruining the finish of many interesting documentary pieces in the acid of the stripping tank. Fortunately, with more general interest in the conservation of good, original paint, such treatment is now rare, and dealers have become more aware of their responsibility to objects that have their own place in furniture history.

When pine first became synonymous with fashionable interiors in the flower-power years it was considered a temporary phenomenon, like the pastel-painted bedroom suites of the 1920s. Instead, what was thought of as a short-lived trend has become one of the fastest growth areas of the antique and furniture trades, with its own specialist shops and manufacturers. Some work in traditional style only, recreating such skilled copies of Irish dressers

OPPOSITE *Ornate carved pine was usually gilded to conceal the wood when it was used in great houses. This pier glass, in the manner of Benjamin Goodison, was made c.1745.*

ABOVE *In most parts of the United States pine was readily available and was used for furniture of all qualities. The simple functionalism of this early 18th-century desk reveals an elegance of design stemming from an uncomplicated use of simple materials.*

RIGHT A pine 'maid's box' was a necessary piece of kitchen equipment in British homes until the 1920s. A divided removable tray held cleaning substances, with dusters and brushes kept in the lower compartment. Many were originally painted; c.1890.

BELOW A Swedish writing box decorated in the folk manner with painted roses. It was originally a gift from a young man to his fiancée and is dated 1806. It comes from the Vingaker parish in Sodermanland.

or American dower chests that their products are often mistaken for genuine antiques. Others specialize in modern pieces or adapt original designs to contemporary interiors, enabling them to fit a kitchen or panel a dining room in any style from 'Adam' to French Provincial. In its cheapest form, pine furniture is available from mail-order catalogues, chain stores and small furniture shops, so there are few homes without a piece or two.

As pine was such an economical wood in the 18th and 19th centuries, it was not associated with the work of any of the great cabinetmakers or schools of progressive design. It was always the wood of the people, used mainly for everyday furniture whose forms had evolved gradually. While modern craftsmen are proud to mark their work, antique examples are rarely attributable and when, for instance, a painted chest carries decorative initials, they are those of the owner rather than the maker. As a consequence, the development of pine furniture has to be studied in relation to the areas where it was made and the changing uses to which it was put. In each

country there were indigenous methods of decoration and different ways of storing food or protecting valuable textiles, all of which tend to influence the native craftsmen working in the traditional manner.

Because most decorators now concentrate on creating a look or an atmosphere rather than attempting a museum-like reconstruction using only completely original pieces, some modern as well as antique examples are included. As the mood of an interior is often derived from a particular region or period, rooms of different dates and from many countries have been included, both to provide inspiration for settings and to give some concept of the limitless possibilities of furnishing with pine. The reasons why particular forms were popular, the methods of restoring original examples, how to care for and select fine pieces, all are discussed. The problem of authenticity is invariably of concern when purchases are made as an investment, so methods of spotting deliberate fakes are highlighted to provide the enthusiast with enough knowledge to buy antique or modern pine with confidence.

ABOVE *Library fittings in Gothic taste, constructed for Marks Hall in Colchester, Essex, England, a 1750s mansion. The pine was originally oak grained but had been painted many times before the house was demolished in the 1950s.*

THE DEVELOPMENT OF PINE FURNITURE

VERY EARLY EXAMPLES of pine furniture are rare, since the wood is by nature soft and susceptible to damage. As some species grew abundantly in Northern Europe, pinewoods were used from the earliest time alongside oak, which was much more durable. The simplest method of creating a piece of furniture, such as a chair or a cradle, was to gouge out the shape from a section of tree trunk, an ancient technique whose influence is discernible in European and American country furniture.

In Great Britain, pine was rarely used before the Restoration (1660), but because of deforestation and the subsequent shortage of native woods, huge quantities were later imported from Europe. The Fire of London in 1666 and the consequent rebuilding and refurbishing, mainly in softwoods, resulted in such an increase in the use of foreign woods that it was said that the Norwegians were very happy to warm themselves by the Fire of London.

Though generally grouped together by sellers of furniture under the now-fashionable term 'pine', there are in fact 70 to 100 different species of pinewood in the Northern temperate zones and the mountains of the Tropics. Conifer woods provide most of the timber that is used today, as the trees grow well in plantations. Fast-grown timber is used mainly for constructional work as it has wider growth rings and large knots, which make it unsuitable for furniture. Slowly grown, mature wood with narrow, regular growth rings is used for good furniture, as it is more easily worked and takes a finer finish.

As some of the ancient pines could grow to 180 ft (55m) with a diameter of as much as 54 in (1m 37cm), the wood became all-important in the American and Canadian furniture trades and was used for the homes of both rich and poor. In the United States, yellow pine (*Pinus strobus*) was most frequently used for furniture as it is even-textured, with little visual difference between the sapwood around the edges of the trunk and the heartwood in the centre. Because it was excellent for joinery, Lord Weymouth made great efforts to grow the tree in Great Britain in the early 18th century, hence its popular title, 'Weymouth Pine'.

Pitch pine grows well in the southern United States and since it is hard, dense and close-textured, it is mainly employed in construction work and flooring, although it is increasingly used for rustic furniture. Its dark heartwood, strongly defined bands of winter and summer growth, and its generally coarse texture were not attractive to the 19th-century joiners who sought a more even effect. Today, because of the interest in folk-style interiors and an acceptance of less sophisticated surfaces, pitch pine has become fashionable.

In Europe, Scots pine (or Baltic redwood) is found in almost every Northern country, although it reaches its greatest height in the coldest areas such as Norway, Sweden and Russia. It was traditional to use Scots pine (*Pinus sylvestris*) for house carpentry or where a wood capable of withstanding damp or actual water was needed. The slow-grown mature timber with narrow

OPPOSITE *An interesting and unusual bookcase, constructed in the manner of a bureau, but with three slope-front drawers instead of the bureau flap. English-made, c.1780.*

ABOVE *American pine was frequently grained, as in this 19th-century looking glass from Pennsylvania. The frame has fluted columns and has yellow graining painted on a red ground. The small painted panel is in naive folk style.*

growth rings and small knots, such as was found in the ancient Swedish and German forests, was best for furniture making, but very high quality wood of this type is rarely available today. As younger woods are so charged with turpentine and resinous matter, they are difficult to work and were avoided by the early craftsmen, who selected the better mature woods for their more expensive products.

Most furniture makers before the mid 19th century bought their timber 'in the log' from importers. Large stocks of pine were not maintained, as the wood tended to split if it was kept too long. When selecting timber, the Victorian craftsman was advised to look for a fir log with the ends dry, firm and free from any evidence of softness or the resinous streaks that would spoil the surface of planks. Any log that exhibited twisted growth was to be avoided, because the planks would shrink and twist even further as they dried out. 'Shakes', cracks that followed the grain, were particularly unsuited to furniture making, as was any tree with gnarled growth and many knots.

Unlike the furniture buyers of today, who appreciate knotty pine, 19th-century joiners saw these marks as imperfections. Frequently, the knot would be cut right out of the plank and a neat rectangle of clean wood inserted so that the surface would be uniform. This technique was often used on furniture that was to be painted or grained, and it is only when the piece is stripped that the inserts are revealed. As furniture dried, it was not unusual for the centre of the knot to fall out, so that the practice of 'patching' the wood had a functional as well as a decorative motivation.

As timber merchants took over the purchase of imported consignments 'in the log', craftsmen were free to select planks of wood for the work in hand. The cheapest type of white pine, known as deal, was originally from the Baltic States and Friesland, its name being evolved from Low German. It was exported in planks that were 7–11 ins (17–28 cm) wide and 3¼ in (8.25 cm) thick. These large pieces, known as 'deals', were from 18–22 ft (5.5–6.7m) long. Shorter lengths were known as 'deal ends' or 'battens'. Any boards that were wider than 11 in (28 cm) were described as 'planks' and attracted a heavier duty. Deal was used extensively for cheaper furniture, despite the presence of hard veins that often protruded above the surface. As it invariably shrinks, no matter how much care is taken in drying, it was not a good surface for veneer. In the Victorian period, certain thicknesses were used for specific purposes: ¾ in (2 cm), for instance, was used for bed bottoms, while 1¼ in (3 cm) was used for tenter frames that were covered with the hangings and did not require great strength.

Some good quality pine furniture was used in Great Britain alongside oak: one 16th-century description mentions a 'table of fine deale'. In general, the better early pieces were of German, Austrian or Spanish origin but are nowadays extremely rare as pine has been lightly considered in comparison to more expensive woods; we have to presume, then, that many pieces were discarded once their designs became unfashionable.

Norway was the largest European supplier of pine by the early 18th century, and it was at that time that developments in the commercialization

ABOVE *The vast amount of linen used in the 19th century necessitated large shelved storage cupboards. This massive British housekeeper's cupboard in pitch pine was constructed in one piece for a country house.*

of furniture production became significant. Machines for making joints, for planing and fluting, and for grooving and tonguing boards became common by the end of the century, thus enabling the middle classes to own much more sophisticated furniture. The wood was worked by carpenters and joiners, whose areas of specialization were governed by guild rules. In Great Britain and the United States, whose small towns had few craftsmen, guild rules were relaxed, but they were strictly imposed in Germany, where crafts often remained within families. In general, joiners were responsible for the finer work, while the carpenters constructed utilitarian commissions such as kitchen shelves or deal tables for taverns.

In the peasant homes of Northern Europe, where the whole family often lived, worked and slept in a single room, the walls were lined with an assortment of pine shelves, benches and cupboards. Sleeping benches and

ABOVE *Some reproduction pine is constructed to higher specifications than old examples. This contemporary bureau fits well into a reception room or a bedroom, as the warm colour of pine adapts to varied colour schemes and styles of decoration.*

beds were accommodated in cupboards and storage areas were fitted under tables and chairs, so that not an inch of space was lost. In richer homes, these fittings were craftsman-made, but poorer people made the more basic pieces themselves or employed a carpenter, so the quality of workmanship is very wide. The peasants of Sweden and Poland took great pride in their household furnishings, and there was a spirit of competition over the complexity of decoration that proved family wealth.

The British country dweller, free from the rigid traditions that governed peasant life in the rest of Europe, exhibited much less interest in the home. Whereas the Northern peasants were forced, because of long winters, to spend much of their time indoors, the British regarded furniture in a much

more functional way and therefore their pieces have little painted ornamentation or detailed carving. Unlike the peasants of Russia or Norway, Britons had no firmly established tradition of furniture design or lifestyle, and basic country homes were frequently sparsely furnished. Furniture styles were much influenced by London fashions, and the more prosperous country people were eager to decorate their homes in imitation of those of the professional classes. The boundary between country and town taste is, consequently, much less defined than in Continental Europe.

American pine furniture is more varied in construction than that found in any other country. Avidly collected since the 1920s, pine can be thought of as a colourful reflection of the origins and development of a nation. The

ABOVE *Pine at its simplest and most functional is seen in the living room of a traditional East Karelian house from Finland. In Border Karelia the dining table was set in the centre of the room with its head to the rear wall. The benches are yellow painted. On the right is a cradle and a baby walker.*

RIGHT *A cut-work Swedish 'wool basket' dating to the Middle Ages. The open-work cutting is typical of traditional folk work.*

TOP *A late 18th-century English pedestal stand with an interior shelved cupboard. Such pieces were used for candelabra, a lamp or a perfume burner. Many were originally painted or grained and were sometimes plaster-decorated to match other architectural fittings.*

ABOVE *Most of the larger children's toys were made of pine in the 18th and 19th centuries. This American sledge, dating to the late 19th century, has stencilled decoration in black on the grained sides and painted decoration that includes the American eagle on the seat.*

almost constant flood of immigrant craftsmen resulted in a rich variety of woodworking methods and decorative skills, providing the buyer of today with an extremely wide choice. As people from Europe favoured particular regions of North America, they retained many of the traditions of their grandparents, reconstructing virtual copies of the peasant homes they had left behind. Even today, Americans with Swedish or German roots will seek to furnish their homes with antique pieces from their country of origin. A number of craftsmen work in the traditional European country manner, so that a pine kitchen, for instance, can be provided in almost any idiom.

German influence was particularly strong in Philadelphia where, in 1850, there were some 725 German furniture craftsmen, most of these originating from the south and perpetuating the designs of their homeland. In New York and Pennsylvania, Dutch influence was considerable, and the cabinets and hanging cupboards made of plain and painted pine are reminiscent of the Swedish-made 'best kitchens' that were the pride of every household in the Netherlands. Many of the Scandinavian and German immigrants who settled in Minnesota travelled with their possessions packed in painted or carved pine chests that were to become family heirlooms – and among the most desirable of all American antiques.

Despite the influence of Swedish, Dutch and German craftsmen, it was British design that exerted the strongest influence on commercially made American furniture, as it was to English pattern books that the fashionable turned for ideas. Since pine was the cheapest wood, it was used to copy desks, cupboards and side tables that were originally conceived in walnut or mahogany. Many items were painted in order to disguise the wood and country makers added a date in European peasant tradition.

While a folk-type painted blanket chest was acceptable in a country house, the smart townsfolk of the New World demanded more sophisticated furniture that spelled success: gilded side tables, mahogany bedroom suites and ormolu display cabinets. It was not until the passion for folk art and primitive design which had begun in Europe in the late 19th century reached the United States that regional country furniture came into its own. As antique examples are now so scarce, interior decorators are offered a wide selection of reproductions, some so cleverly aged and distressed that they can become a trap for the unwary.

The manner of working pinewoods underwent a complete change in the 18th century because of the fashion for painted and gilded furniture. Since the wood was obscured by the surface finish, it was unnecessary to use expensive woods such as mahogany or walnut, and interior decorators and cabinetmakers in Europe and America began to employ softwood for chimneypieces, panelling, side tables and pedestals. As pine was looked down upon by richer people, it was disguised in various ways and made to resemble substances as diverse as tortoiseshell and marble.

Despite the fact that pine is not ideally suited for intricate carving, some delicate items, such as candle sconces and wall brackets, were made. Occasionally, when the surface gilding was beyond repair these pieces were stripped and waxed, and they now provide some concept of the top-class work that was possible in the medium. Superb breakfront bookcases, classical-style library shelves, elegant corner cupboards with broken pediments and 'my lady's' toilet table' were all made in softwood – though of course its humble identity was never revealed.

When the surface gilding or paint became chipped or badly marked, the fittings were often repainted, and it is not unusual to find an 18th-century Adam-style piece with as many as six different treatments, ranging from Victorian oak graining to a coating of the pale green favoured in the 1920s. In such circumstances, it is almost impossible to simulate the original finish, and the pieces are stripped and waxed to reveal the quality of workmanship. Pine furniture of this type is now highly desirable as it holds its own in any surroundings, but it is inevitably quite expensive.

Fortunately, decorators can recreate a style with reproductions, although even then the cost can be considerable since furniture of this quality demands a high degree of craftsmanship. Completely panelled rooms, library shelves and Adam-style sideboards and pedestals are available today, so that the warmth of pine can be combined with the 18th-century elegance which has always remained popular. In the United States, it is possible to purchase 'classical pine' of this type in construction-kit form, although the manufacturers concentrate on smaller pieces such as desks and side tables. Panelling and columns to line a complete room are available from specialist suppliers in most countries.

The medieval tradition of using native woods for furniture making was completely disregarded in the 19th century, despite the protestations of artist-craftsmen, who believed that it was only by working with indigenous

ABOVE *Good quality, well-seasoned pine can be carved in great detail. This northern Italian candle bracket dates to the 17th century and is painted. It is from a set of twenty-four especially made for one of the great Italian families. The horseman in the central plaque probably relates to the family coat of arms.*

LEFT Living with pine was taken to its ultimate in the log cabins of Canada and North America. In this pioneer cabin in North Dakota, painted pine was used for the plain tables, shelves and chairs which were constructed locally.

BELOW A Federal long-case clock made in Connecticut. It was painted by R Cole who stencilled 'R Cole Painter' on the base in gold. The hinged door centres a stencilled compote with fruit; c.1825.

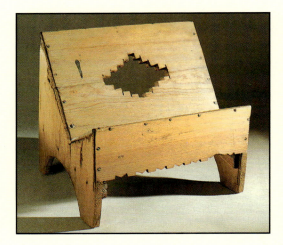

TOP *American Shaker furniture was always simple and made to reveal the intrinsic beauty of material. This three-step stool, for a high bed or a library, was made in New Lebanon in New York State and dates to 1830.*

ABOVE *The stands that supported heavy family or church bibles were often made of pine in country districts, though the cheap wood was sometimes concealed with paint. This missal stand comes from Morada in New Mexico and was made c.1900.*

materials that near-perfection could be achieved. The strictures of significant men like Charles Lock Eastlake and William Morris had little influence on commercial furniture production, as the public demanded novelty rather than craftsmanship. Improvements in communications meant that the products of Canada and the Baltic States were always available, so pinewoods became, as they are today, the mainstay of international furniture production.

As the middle classes became more prosperous and working people took a greater interest in the furnishing of their homes, marketing began to change. There was an increase in the number of large stores where rooms were set out and dozens of different suites and chairs were displayed. In small towns, and some villages, there were furniture retailers who offered products from a variety of suppliers and even from different countries. Although local carpenters frequently supplied functional items such as kitchen tables and benches, the bulk of 19th-century pine was sold through shops or mail-order catalogues, the latter very necessary in a country such as the United States, where so many people lived in remote areas.

The late 19th-century furniture shops were packed with suites of every description made to suit every pocket. Identical designs were often available in several woods, of which deal was always the cheapest. This was usually grained, stained or painted to make it more impressive. Some surprisingly strong colours, such as bright reds and blues, were used for bedroom suites around 1900, although cream enamel was most popular, especially for servants, rooms. In the 1870s and 1880s, satin black and various ebonized finishes were liked, while green stain enjoyed a spate of popularity in the 1890s. All these finishes tended to chip and there was frequent repainting, so detail is often obscured under layers of colour.

Because of the proliferation of books on decorating and the magazines that advertised and illustrated the newest fashions, furniture design became much more international in character, and it is often difficult to be sure if a simple suite originated in Germany or Great Britain. Despite the steady increase in commercial production, most manufacturers remained small and sold their work through the many shops and trade warehouses. As some of this furniture often had to be transported over long distances it was an advantage if it was not too heavy. The struggle to produce ever-cheaper pieces for the lower end of the market also resulted in the construction of much lighter work, with the backs of washstands and wardrobes made of the thinnest board available.

In Germany and Scandinavia, plain waxed pine remained popular alongside the various painted finishes, although it was often embellished with stencilled decoration in blue or green. Since Dutch and German housewives used their kitchens as places of display, there was a much greater variety of pine fittings in these countries – such as egg cupboards and china racks – that were sold in natural finishes. Although few complete kitchens have survived, it is possible to study the variety of fittings by examining the miniature versions that were supplied as teaching toys for little girls.

After 1865, machinery began to be used extensively for fashionable commercial furniture, and mechanical twisting lathes were developed as well as devices for cutting curves and carving. The shaping of legs, fret-cutting and incising could all be carried out mechanically, so there was a great increase in the amount of ornamentation that was applied to cheap furniture. After the introduction of each type of machine-made decoration, there was a fairly short-lived rush to experiment with the new possibilities. When spindle-turning by steam power made bobbin shapes cheap to produce, they appeared by the hundred on dressers, settles, desks and occasional tables.

Much late Victorian and Edwardian furniture is now stripped and waxed to reveal its original workmanship, which although machine-made is often highly decorative. Washstands, bookcases and display cupboards of this type form the basic stock of many dealers in old pine, who often add brass fittings to complement the warm shades of the wood.

ABOVE Traditional styles are now popular for kitchens and pine remains a favourite because of its attractive colours. Knots and heavy graining are no longer concealed with paint or stain but are appreciated as a feature of the wood.

CHESTS
AND
COFFERS

THERE IS SOMETHING irresistibly mysterious about a chest, reminiscent of the treasure and adventure of childhood stories, or the excitement when the hero of a detective novel pushed open a creaking lid to discover some unspeakable horror within. A chest is frequently the first piece of antique furniture to be purchased, as it looks effective in any surroundings and is available in a wide price range. For a child's room, a plain blanket chest or a metal-bound trunk will provide adequate storage space for toys and books and can be integrated into any decorative scheme with ease.

The terms 'coffer' and 'chest' are used alongside one another to describe this most ancient piece of furniture, which has never gone completely out of fashion. Chests fit in almost any period home and look dramatic when placed against plain brickwork or metal panels in ultra-modern settings. When domestic furniture was at its most mannered, in the 18th century, this useful piece, although old-fashioned, did not disappear, and the addition of elegant stands gave a more sophisticated, delicate look. Once antique furniture began to be appreciated and collected in the early 19th century, ancient carved chests were frequently displayed in wealthy households as objects of interest and importance. Because of this popularity they were soon re-

OPPOSITE A small coffer with incised and carved decoration, made in the 16th century in Western Finland. It shows the lovely patination of really old pine.

ABOVE Flat and convex topped coffers were stood against the walls in impressive rows in Swedish 'chest rooms', where they were used for the storage of expensive textiles. These marriage chests are all dated and carry the bride's initials.

examples which were mentioned in wills and household inventories.

clothes and possessions increased in number, people often owned several become quite common by this time and were exported all over Europe. As termed 'spruce coffers' or 'Danzig chests'. Baltic fir chests seem to have 16th century, references to pine chests become more specific as they were merchant homes they contained blankets and household equipment. In the carried with them when they visited great houses or castles, while in boxes were used for transporting the furs and costly textiles that the nobility became interchangeable. In the medieval period, strongly made chests and indicated a small chest that might be used for jewellery, but the terms soon the storage of books and plate. In the Middle Ages, the term 'coffer' often

The most ancient chests are made of oak and were used in churches for great popularity of the wood and the value of the finest examples.

shop is as likely to be a fake as any other type of old furniture, reflecting the and birds have been reproduced. Today, the pine coffer seen in an antiques chests were 'improved', although the painted examples with bright flowers authenticity by the addition of an early date. Fortunately, few plain pine assembled from sections of old panelling and furniture and given pseudo-

Carved chests were so coveted by Victorian decorators that they were able in Northern Europe and America.

produced, a trade that gained momentum after folk art became very desir-

As articles of trade were packed in chests for shipping, there was considerable commercial production of cheap pine containers, principally in Russia. These functional items were made in several areas, but especially in Kholmogory, where they were fitted with metal bands for added strength. The surface of the Baltic fir coffers was left plain if they were to be used as packing cases, but painted or skin-covered if intended for personal use.

In Sweden, the earliest examples were made without lids, but by the 16th century the tops were strengthened with metal bands. The construction of Swedish coffers is fairly simple; they comprise plank sides or a few inset panels. In the 18th century, when they were treated as objects of great importance in peasant households, the lids were convex. They were mainly used for the storage of the valuable embroidered textiles that every family owned. Metal carrying handles and locks were fitted and the chests stood on bracket or bun feet. As the coffers often rested on earth floors the feet were necessary to keep the contents free of damp. Domed lids, highly fashionable in northern and southern Sweden, were less popular in the central provinces, where a plain flat top was common.

In richer households, every person owned at least one chest, identified by initials and the date. They were stored in special Chest Rooms where they stood in a line against the walls as evidence of prosperity. They were such an important feature of peasant life that they were constructed in all sizes and in a range of quality. They contained each person's church clothes as well as general household textiles. The bride's chest was important and by the time of the marriage was filled with embroidered festival hangings.

BELOW The painted finish of this chest was intended to represent a clouded type of marble and the design incorporates the date '1813'. The dark blue colouring is typical of the Järusö Parish in Halsingland, Sweden.

ABOVE *An American
blanket chest, made in New
England between 1740 and
1760. Chests of this construction,
with drawers beneath the storage
well, are known in Britain as
'mule chests'. This blue-painted
example stands on the original
turned feet and has the original
brasswork.*

Medieval Swedish chests sometimes have incised decoration derived from cursive Viking ornament, but by the late 18th century painting was more usual. Bold designs, spread across the whole front, are fairly common, but where the surface is divided by metal bands or panels, the patterns are sectionalized. Some chests were left plain except for a delicate garland of flowers that encircled the owner's initials, but the most prized versions are heavily ornamented, with the decoration extending inside the lid.

In Hungary, the bridal chest assumed even greater importance, as it formed part of the Wedding Day rituals of both peasants and nobility. From her earliest days, the girl, with help from her mother, embroidered the fine and colourful hangings that would one day be used for her own home. On the day of her marriage, the dowry chest, by this time packed with her work, was carried in procession to the courtyard of the bridegroom. As all eyes were upon the bride's possessions, the painters made these pine coffers as beautiful as possible.

Bridal chests made for the great Hungarian families were more heavily constructed than those of the peasants and carried the coat of arms as well as the girl's initials. Occasionally, dower chests are found with two sets of initials, indicating that the piece was used by two generations. Highly decorated chests became increasingly popular in the 18th century, although production was at its peak around 1850. In comparison with the bright colours and detailed painting of the later periods, some of the very early bridal chests seem restrained, since their only ornamentation is often the girl's initials, set in a simple carved or incised scroll.

In Germany, the ravages of war meant that little early country furniture survived, as in periods of great turmoil it is the quality items that are saved in preference to the interesting but common possessions of the middle and peasant classes. Some concept of the furnishing of a typical middle-class house can be gained from inventories and wills, although precise details are not given. A more accurate picture is provided by the contents of 17th- and 18th-century dollhouses, precise miniaturizations of merchant houses and made for adult appreciation rather than child's play. In the servants' bedrooms are found plain board chests, devoid of any ornamentation and intended for the storage of clothes. They stand on bracket or bun feet, but those in the kitchens and storage areas are not raised off the floor and were obviously of such a practical nature that they needed no ornamentation.

In Austria and Germany, folk art was influenced to a much greater extent by the fashions of Italy and France. Chests were made in great variety for all classes of society, the more sophisticated examples showing rococo and baroque styles. As the ruling princes had their own court workshops where foreign craftsmen were employed, current fashions were adapted to local tastes, and carpenters were exposed to more progressive work, which encouraged them to create furniture in the mainstream of European design.

The most characteristic German form of chest has a flat lid, wide stiles and panelled ends. These coffers first appeared in the 13th century and were known as 'stollen chests', the word meaning a support post or foot. They were especially liked in the Renaissance, when some of the larger versions assumed almost architectural proportions. In the south of the country, where

ABOVE *A painted blanket chest, made in the United States. The front is painted with three arched panels; the centre panel with the name 'John Seltzer 1799'. A school of Pennsylvania-German chest decorators was active in Lebanon County, New York State, c.1800. Seltzer, a woodworker as well as a painter, was one of those who signed and dated his work.*

27

LEFT The American Shaker community believed in purity of line and shunned ornamentation. In this typical Shaker room, the furniture, though austere, has a beauty of line that is lost when pine is heavily carved or painted. The chest of drawers has pine sides but cherry wood was used for the front and top. The oval chip wood boxes have lids and bases of pine and there is a pine coffer.

they were constructed in softwood, they were usually painted or decorated with an inlay. Few examples of this period come on the market, although reproductions are available for people wishing to recreate the atmosphere of an impressive merchant house.

Wainscot chests also originated in richer households in the 15th century, where they provided seating as well as storage. This style could well be adapted for modern kitchens and dining rooms as the chests are within the ability of any local carpenter. They were built into country interiors in Europe long after they had gone out of fashion. When used in peasant cottages and painted with leaves and flowers in the Bavarian manner, they acted as colourful features in the dark interiors.

In country areas of Germany, especially the Berchtesgaden region where Swiss and Austrian influence was strong, a number of characteristic rustic styles evolved from the ancient plank construction. The chest itself was sometimes suspended within four plank legs, a method that gave additional protection to the storage section and provided the painter with smooth, plain surfaces on which to work. More complex designs with stepped bases and convex tops were used in richer households, and were also painted with flowers and figures. Small decorative panels were fitted to the bases of the finer chests, each painted with a different design.

BELOW *An early 18th-century American blanket chest that stands on bracket feet. It has fielded panels decorated with geometric patterns.*

The simplest method of creating an ornate chest base was to cut a complicated curved and scrolled outline from a narrow plank and apply this to the lower edge. This somewhat rococo-style base could then be painted in imitation of the carved effects seen on more expensive furniture. Many of these painted pine coffers carry the owner's initials and sometimes the date. Even when the painter was working on flat boards, the surface was divided into sections that resembled panels. The most expensive products had arched inset panels and carved bracket or bun feet: such pieces would have been found in the homes of merchants, as in Germany the upper middle classes did not ape the furnishings of princes but continued to equip their houses with practical and colourful furniture with roots in their folk ancestry.

Contemporary interest in painted pine furniture and the folk art of the Alpine regions has encouraged a substantial production of modern work in the traditional idiom. Since the late Victorian period, tourists have returned from Oberammergau or St Ulrich with painted pine chests, some of which have aged so convincingly that they appear to be much older. As tourism was so much a feature of Bavarian life, a considerable amount of furniture was especially made for this market, as well as pieces for domestic use in north Germany, where the style was associated with the romance of Old Germany and the princely states.

Today, pine chests and smaller boxes can be purchased in the white wood, to be painted at home from designs that are supplied in sheet form. Craft publications also give instructions on how to make old-style peasant chests, using 'antique' metal fittings to give a country look. This folk-type painting is now so popular in Germany that instructions are included in women's magazines, making it possible for anyone to own a modern version of this traditional piece.

Because so many people from the Northern European countries emigrated to the United States in the 19th century, the traditions of their native lands were perpetuated in the culture of the New World. Although the

ABOVE *Chests of this construction were found in almost all British homes until the 1920s. They were sometimes used for travelling and were often painted black. When stripped and waxed they are ideal for use as blanket chests or toy boxes.*

wedding processions and much of the ritual connected with the bridal chests of Norway and Hungary were discontinued, the idea of storing linen and needlework for the future home was encouraged. As European customs were dispersed among the population, the dower chest became a feature of many American homes.

From the time an American girl learned to sew, she began to make pieces for her dower chest, its contents revealing how her skills as a needle-woman had developed. Her chest contained items of a practical nature such as sheets and pillowcases, rather than the ornamental cushions and hangings brought out only for special occasions that characterized the European peasant versions.

As pine was so readily available in America, most dower chests were made of this wood, which was often painted for additional protection. Many were constructed by immigrant craftsmen, and they exhibit the strong European influences that evolved into characteristic regional styles still perpetuated today. The dower chests were kept in a place of honour in the girl's family home and she was encouraged to show her neatly stitched work to visitors. The majority measure between 3–4 ft (90–120 cm) long, and a few contain one or two drawers fitted along the lower edge, although this was not common.

The simplest dower chests are of plank construction, but finer examples have fielded panels and convex tops. In order to protect the linen from insects and damp, the chests were raised off the ground on ball or bracket feet; occasionally, a trestle device is found. The painted decoration is sometimes confined to the rectangular or arched panels, with the remainder left as plain wood, but many were completely covered with ornament. As in Europe, it was common to add the girl's initials and the date.

While it is romantic to think that the dower chests were made and decorated within the home, the vast majority were the work of professional carpenters and joiners, working in the style of their native country. The decoration was the work of itinerant painters who visited the remotest areas and sometimes used stencils to speed up the process. Fortunately, the chests were always highly regarded and have survived within families in some number.

Reproduction chests of this type are now found in many regions, and especially in Pennsylvania, where the German influence is so strong. They are used as storage furniture in bedrooms, kitchens and halls, and add a touch of glowing colour to a dark area.

Apart from the dower chests that are especially associated with the United States, many simpler designs developed from within the community, and there was much homemade furniture from the early settlers. Unfortunately, very little of this homestead work has survived, as it was discarded once the family could afford commercially made pieces. The plain pine chests of the settlers now hold great appeal because of the affection for rural crafts, and examples are found in the stock of exclusive shops specializing in primitive and folk art. This early furniture, often made with only two or three tools, can now command high prices as buyers feel they are acquiring a piece of American history.

British country people also kept their possessions in chests, but these were far more prosaic structures than those found in the parts of Europe where the peasants took such pleasure in display. A comparable pride in the decoration of the home did not develop strongly in Great Britain until the 19th century, when the lower classes began to enjoy higher wages and wanted to display their new-found relative prosperity. Despite the lack of highly ornamented chests, the examples that survive are notable for their robust country style and can look especially effective when seen in combination with modern furniture. As some designs and manufacturing methods

ABOVE A *Shropshire country coffer, made c.1795, with plank panels set within shaped mouldings. The legs are extensions of the stiles. It has a central lock and the pine was originally oak grained.*

ABOVE A *blanket box with simple moulded decoration and cast iron carrying handles. A type that was originally used for travelling.*

changed so little in remote areas from one generation to the next, individual examples are difficult to date precisely.

English chests of the medieval period were almost invariably made of oak and those intended for wealthy households or churches were heavily carved. The complexity of such pieces led to the formation of the Guild of Cofferers in the 14th century, a group responsible for the finest carved works, such as dower chests owned by young noblewomen. Some of the medieval chests were painted, but these, like the heavily carved versions, disappeared as chests became less of a necessity in the homes of the rich.

The amount of Flemish furniture, especially chests, that was being imported in the 15th century alarmed British craftsmen, as prices were much lower than for comparable native work. The softwood fir coffers known as 'Dansk', or Danish, chests became a feature of many households, where they were used for the storage of books, plate and textiles. Some were covered with velvet, leather or skin, and became ornamental features of the bedchambers of richer people. Smaller covered chests of this type never went completely out of fashion, and were still made in the late Victorian period, when the cheapest versions were papered in imitation of metal banding and studding.

Framed chests were so labour-intensive that they were inevitably expensive, and 18th-century versions are much harder to find than the plank types that could be put together by any local carpenter. The plainest have solid sides, but the effect of feet was often given by cutting away a triangular wedge. Such constructions are usually known as 'six plank chests', although in fact the sides were made from the fifth plank cut in half. The majority were originally painted, and when sold stripped, they have lost such additions as the original lining papers that often help in their dating.

Making framed chests involved the cutting of a number of mortise and tenon joints, as well as the grooves for panels, and demanded much greater skill. In order to save work, a number were made with plain plank sides. Those that incorporate a number of panels, preferably of different sizes, are the most desirable, although a plain lid is often favoured by the interior decorator as it provides a better surface for lamps or ornaments. Sometimes square and rectangular panels are combined or a line of very small panels will border the upper or lower edge. Such examples are among the most expensive pine coffers since they often exhibit excellent craftsmanship.

Many chests made before 1830 contain a small compartment that was intended for candles. These rectangular boxes are fixed to the left of the coffers just inside the lid, so that the candles could be found easily. It was believed that tallow candles acted as a moth repellent, especially useful where woollen blankets were stored. Many candle boxes are found with missing or replacement lids, although this does not affect the value very greatly as they were obviously subjected to considerable wear.

The idea of including drawers in the lower section of a chest was developed because of the problem of finding objects in those which were very deep. The so-called 'mule chests' first appeared *c* 1650 and pointed the

way towards the manufacture of chests of drawers which eventually ousted the coffer from country bedrooms. When the use of chests was revived in the late Victorian period, they became the province of artist-craftsmen who were seeking to revive the honesty of early country furniture and looked to the medieval period for inspiration.

Many of the pine chests now found in the stock of antiques dealers were originally used for travel and have cheap, cast-iron carrying handles. When sanded and polished, these can look surprisingly effective and provide both storage space in a kitchen or bedroom and occasional seating. These plain rectangular boxes, sometimes with metal bands, were made in all sizes, from massive versions intended for an officer travelling to India on a long posting to the small tuckboxes that were sent to children at school. They were so strongly made that they have survived in some number alongside the similarly constructed pine blanket chests used in most European and American homes until central heating made the storage of a large quantity of blankets unnecessary.

ABOVE *An English 18th-century plank-sided coffer with its original brass lock plate. Inside there is a candle box with a lid.*

SEAT
FURNITURE

PINE SEATING FOR KITCHENS and dining rooms is popular, since it provides a light, relaxed country atmosphere, redolent of wholesome foods and the smell of freshly baked bread. As so little skilled craftsmanship was needed for the construction of benches, antique and modern versions are similar, unless the wood has been smothered with varnish, which gives a hard, unnatural look. A much greater degree of skill was needed for the manufacture of chairs; very fine examples in unpainted pine are rare due to the general popularity of other woods.

Many chairs and benches were originally painted or grained and the makers used several different woods in their construction. For strength, hardwoods such as oak or elm were frequently employed for the legs of pine-seated kitchen chairs that were to be grained and varnished, but these can look very ugly when the pieces are stripped and the differences in colour revealed. Some panelled settles were also made from badly matched or different woods, therefore anyone purchasing a rough item for stripping is advised to check the construction well before paying a high price.

In medieval halls – where benches were the commonest type of seating – plank legs, either left plain or cut in cursive outline, provided strong side supports. Pine seating was quite common in Europe but was not recorded in Great Britain until the 15th century, when pieces were imported from the Netherlands and known as 'Flanders forms'. The simplest method of providing back support for someone sitting on a bench was to place it against the wainscot. In the town houses of German merchants, built-in seating of this type was usually painted and the benches ran around the complete room. In wealthy 16th-century households, turned legs, which gave a lighter effect, were more popular, although plank supports were common in country houses both large and small. Long after wainscot benches were forgotten in fashionable interiors, they continued to be a feature of peasant homes, as they were the ideal method of accommodating a number of people in a small space.

Pine benches were sometimes made more decorative by the addition of shaped underframing, which also gave extra strength to the construction and helped to avoid the possibility of the long seat warping. Bracket side-supports were sensible, as the benches could be taken apart and stored away when not required. Cushions and upholstery helped make the forms a little more comfortable, but are rarely used today since they tend to spoil the line unless integral to the construction. An interesting type of bench is recorded in early 17th-century German prints: two heavy stools, enclosed on four sides, were linked with a plank to provide additional seating for banquets.

The construction of a simple bench is within the capacity of most people and they have remained a feature of the country interior from the earliest times, used for seating, as a table at the foot of a bed, or as stands for equipment in the kitchen. Colourful painted reproductions can be purchased in the Alpine regions of Europe and in parts of the United States where German and Scandinavian influence was strong. Plainer versions, ideal on

OPPOSITE *In small peasant homes with limited space, dual purpose furniture was useful. This Irish 18th-century settle bed has shaped plank sides forming simple arms. It is raised from the ground on stepped feet.*

ABOVE *When tilted forward, the seat converts into a box bed that would have been filled with straw or a feather mattress.*

ABOVE *Pine stools are found in country houses of all types in Europe and America. In Hezlett House in Northern Ireland a group is ranged around a peat fire. The pine dresser with a pot board and cut-work frieze, is also typically Irish.*

either side of a long table, can be found in the stock of many dealers and are made in a wide range of quality by contemporary craftsmen.

A settle is differentiated from a bench by the presence of arms. The earliest types have storage space under seats that are lifted. As there were very few chairs in houses or palaces before the late 16th century, the settle, spread with cushions, was one of the most comfortable pieces of furniture. Set under a canopy, the settle became the seat of honour for an important visitor or the head of the household. Like benches, settles were also built-in and were sometimes constructed to continue around a corner with the arms on different walls.

SEAT FURNITURE

In country houses, the settle was always placed near the fire and provided with a high back to stop draughts. Pine versions continued to be made long after this form of seating had gone out of fashion among the wealthy, who used chairs. From the 17th to the late 19th centuries, the design changed very little since settles were made, in the main, for countryfolk. Many of the examples that come on the market were obviously constructed for specific positions and can look ungainly when seen out of their original environment. Some of the most striking have curved panelled backs and two or three compartments in the seats. A simple moulding was used as a top edging, but finer examples have a carved or intricately moulded cornice, occasionally with the refinement of a dentilled edge. Cheaper versions have long, plain panels in the backs and the seats have lift-tops. Cupboards, set into the panelling of the base, are refinements found mainly on better quality pieces. Although large furniture is often difficult to sell, massive pine settles are very popular and look dramatic in dining rooms or large farmhouse-style kitchens.

Settle tables, with backs that fold down onto the arms to form a table, are another ancient design. Known popularly in Great Britain as 'monk's benches', they were useful for serving light meals or for card playing. Pine versions were country-made throughout the 19th century and they enjoyed a

LEFT Ornamental chair backs provided an excellent means of displaying native craftsmanship. The blue-painted chair is dated '1853' and the carved back with a decorative frieze is dated '1812'.

ABOVE 1853 Swedish chair, shown with its plaited straw seat. Stretchers at foot level gave the piece added strength. From the Stävie parish in Skåne.

revival between World Wars I and II, when they were made of stained and grained softwood. These recent examples are often stripped and look much more effective without their original finish.

The need to provide as much storage space as possible in a single piece of furniture resulted in the fitting of cupboards into the backs of settles. Local variations are found in most peasant interiors, especially where the settles form part of the built-in fitments. In Great Britain, where free-standing furniture was common, pieces of this type are known as bacon cupboards and are among the most desirable country items. Inside the long, shallow cupboards were massive hooks for hanging the sides of bacon that were the only

RIGHT *The parlour of the Antti House from Sakyla in Satakunta Province in Finland. The house is symmetrical and a door from a porch on the left leads through an entrance hall to this room with its Empire-style windows. The long trestle tables derive from medieval styles. The room is seen in its every-day state. It would have been decorated with textiles for festivals.*

meat that some poorer families tasted in the winter months. Because settles were positioned near the fire, the cupboards were also used for hanging up coats and keeping them aired. Occasionally, examples with top cupboards that are stepped forward are found; these are especially sought after. In more refined versions, the cupboards in the base are replaced by drawers.

Settle beds, although historically interesting, are not as attractive as the high-backed settles that were often the work of skilled joiners. In general, the beds are found in the poorest areas and are crudely constructed from thick planks. Built-in versions are found all over Europe, most functioning on the principle of an inverted L-shaped seat that tilts to the ground to form a long, narrow box that could be fitted with a mattress or filled with bracken or straw. Such pieces, being rare, would command good prices from museums, although they are not particularly decorative and do not have great appeal for the ordinary buyer.

Although mainly associated with country interiors, pine settles were often used to furnish the kitchens of large houses, so that some beautifully made, panelled versions of massive size are found. They were ideal for work areas, as they were not over-comfortable and did not encourage the servants to sit down for any length of time.

Today, the most frequently found settles are the comparatively low-backed box types that often stand on sledge feet. These are of the simplest construction and have hinged seats for access to the blanket-chest section. Known as 'Welsh cottage' settles in Great Britain, they were found in almost every home in Wales before World War II. As they were produced commercially in such great numbers, they were economically made of thin wood, so that large examples can be surprisingly light. The majority were originally painted or grained, so the makers were not concerned about using different woods. Unfortunately, when stripped, this economy is revealed in an unpleasant patchwork of colour and quality. However, this type of settle is widely available, and the buyer can usually locate a satisfactory specimen.

A bench chest was one of the few moveable items in a French peasant interior, where most of the furniture was fitted. Salt was used in such vast quantity that one type of bench seat was especially designed for the dry storage of this commodity and was always placed near the fire. Unlike in Great Britain and the United States, where there was little fitted pine seating, much European country furniture was the work of the craftsmen who built the houses, and so gave an integrated look that is too often missing from modern homes. This type of construction is seen particularly in Russia, where wall benches were a feature of both palaces and peasant homes. One unusual form of Russian bench, with a raised section for the head, was intended for sleeping. Bed settles of various types are recorded in many parts of Europe but were usually slightly wider versions of the old wainscot types.

'Turn-over settles' are mainly associated with Sweden, and illustrate another method of living neatly in cramped conditions. These settles were heavily constructed, with thick, turned legs and substantial stretchers. They were made more rigid by the addition of a row of turned rails that linked the

ABOVE *Variations on the back-board chair are found in most Northern European countries. This piece, from Sakyla in Finland, dates to the early 18th century and has compass-type ornament in chip carving that relies on the play of light and shadow for its effect.*

lower stretchers to the plank seat. Similarly, turned rails gave additional strength to the backs. Turn-over settles were used on either side of long dining tables, in small rooms. To avoid having to move the settles when the meal was complete, the backs were lifted from a simple groove, then turned over so that they faced away from the table. Simpler settles using this form of construction were made in the 19th century and ornamented with carved or cut-work backs.

In Hungary, some of the pine seat furniture was painted with the initials of the husband and wife, together with their wedding date and, sometimes, the date when the item was made. In openwork benches from northern Hungary, the decoration of the backs often included the figures of hussars, with the date when a young man's military service ended, a time of great family rejoicing that was commemorated in the piece of furniture. In this part of Hungary, the most ornate settles and benches were the work of herdsmen, who included bird and flower devices in their cut-work designs. The complex profile-cutting was displayed against plain colour-washed walls, which threw the patterns into sharp relief. Some of the more complex examples have latticework backgrounds and as many as 10 different panels were used to illustrate stories from the New Testament.

The Hungarian bench carvers decorated their work with scenes from village life, the seasons, episodes on the hunting field and people at their daily work. The benches are now among the finest and most lively examples of European folk art. As the cutting of complex panels was intricate, hardwood was often used for these sections instead of pine, which was more difficult to work. In peasant houses, the settles, both plain and ornamented, were placed side by side around the main living room and made more comfortable with embroidered cushions.

The naïve charm and honesty of the craftsmanship exhibited in peasant and early country furniture were lost in the Victorian period, as industrialization swept away local styles and construction methods. Settles began to be associated with narrow, dark halls, and grained Gothic styles in softwoods were made in large numbers for middle-class houses. Antique styles were favoured by richer, more fashionable people, and there was considerable manufacture of reproduction and fake pieces. The pine Gothic-style settles, made for modest homes, can look very attractive when stripped and polished, and their somewhat ecclesiastical gloom is swept away with rich fabrics and luxurious carpets.

Demolition of old and unwanted chapels and churches inevitably results in the sale of their painted or grained pine pews; which are snapped up by interior decorators for waiting rooms, restaurants, kitchens and dining rooms. These pews have now become so popular that reproductions are produced in order to keep up with demand. Some of these are made in useful shorter sizes for modern houses: while the effect is hardly authentic, they are obviously much better suited in scale.

Almost any type of traditional bench or settle, apart from the cut-work of the Hungarian herdsmen, can be obtained in reproduction, so the

RIGHT *The simplest seat furniture evolved from natural forms as in this early Norwegian fisherman's seat used in the outer archipelago. It is a type of rustic folk furniture that is sometimes reproduced today.*

decorator can select either a regional or national style. Contemporary craftsmen will adapt and modify designs to specification, fitting a settle into an alcove or difficult corner, for example, to become an interesting feature with useful storage space in the base. When good, well-made antique versions cannot be obtained, it is much better to choose a contemporary piece made by a known craftsman rather than a badly made Victorian example that was never intended to be seen without paint.

Even stools were expected to provide additional storage for linen in Swedish peasant homes. These chest-stools are rarely seen outside Sweden and were, in effect, a long, shallow box, usually with a lock, that stood on plain legs. The sides of the chest section were frequently panelled and decorated with flower painting. By definition, a stool is a seat for one person and is always without a back rest. Few early softwood examples have survived, although structures that were almost certainly made of pine appear in medieval paintings. Those with much stronger board sides can be seen in engravings; they were made more decorative by fret-cutting. Four-sided openwork plank stools were popular in German houses in the 17th century, but the commonest form in Europe and the United States was the simple trestle, which has never gone out of fashion.

Three-legged stools were useful in country houses and farms because of their uneven earth or stone floors. They could be made by any home craftsman as the legs did not need to be precisely measured and angled. Low milking stools were always made with three legs, so that the milker could sit securely in the field, and milking stools are often found with round, octagonal or hexagonal seats made of pine, although the legs are usually of ash or hazel. As they were completely functional items, they were crudely made, and the legs were fixed with wedges or a simple tenon. A most unusual one-legged stool was used in Wiltshire fields in England, although examples are most likely to be found in a museum.

Victorian domestic stools, including the painted versions from Northern Europe, are not difficult to find, although very early examples rarely come on the market. Some highly sophisticated pine versions were made in the Grecian and Egyptian manner when painted and gilded furniture became fashionable towards the end of the Georgian period, but these are of such high quality that they would only be stripped in exceptional circumstances. Some items that appear to be stools were originally made as stands for kitchens and store rooms, where they were used for the washing tub or a row of large earthenware jars, for example. Perhaps because they are so functional by nature, plain pine stools still look most effective in the more practical areas of the house.

By adding a back support to a stool, the most basic form of chair was evolved, a development that can be traced in the rudimentary designs of European peasant furniture. In the Middle Ages, chairs were rare even in the great palaces, and were considered a symbol of authority – a tradition that was continued in peasant homes, where the main chair was reserved for important visitors or the head of the household. Box-like chairs with panelled sides and backs were frequently made of pine, as were the simple plank chairs

BELOW In this cut fir stool, the branches, growing naturally from the trunk, served as the legs. Such stools were often used in the small chimneyless dwelling huts inhabited by peasants in Finland.

OPPOSITE *The interior of a Finnish 'chimenyless hut' or 'smoke hut' with a stone stove. It was originally situated in the Pajasyrjä village of Jaakkima and was built c.1826. The furniture is very practical and there is a table side-seat with tree branch legs. There were no beds, as the family slept on the benches or on a straw mattress on the floor. The block-legged table, of early medieval type, is very rare.*

with plain, high backs and outline-cut arms. Few really high quality pine armchairs are known, even though the wood was capable of considerable ornamentation and was painted and gilded by some of the most important cabinetmakers around 1800.

Hall chairs and benches began to be specially made in the Georgian period (1714-1830) and were always associated with antique styles and heraldic ornamentation. Cheap, painted softwood versions in the Gothic taste were made by the thousands for lower-middle-class homes in the late 19th century. Although very uncomfortable because of shields and other devices carved in relief, stripped and waxed examples can look good in areas of the house where they would be rarely used.

The design of Northern European country furniture, which was frequently made of pine, relied on constructions of flat splats that gave the wood added strength. Three-legged forms were very popular and were given plank backs that were cut in decorative outline. Chairs of this design are still made today and, decorated with traditional patterns, can still create the atmosphere of an Alpine chalet.

In Great Britain, many cheap kitchen chairs are described as pine, even though it is often only the seat that was made of that wood. The back rails, legs and stretchers are more often beech or oak, or, in the United States, hickory or maple. Some, despite their assortment of woods, come up well when stripped, but others are a disaster and best repainted or given some traditional type of decorative finish. Matched sets of well-made kitchen chairs, often seen in smart dining rooms, can be quite expensive, although single examples and pairs can be purchased cheaply. In a country-look interior, a variety of different designs can be more interesting than a set, but make sure that each is a good example of its type.

The easiest way of looking after a number of babies and toddlers in a nursery or in the crowded living room of a cottage was to enclose each in a low, almost box-like chair from which escape was difficult. German engravings, dating to the 16th century, show chairs of this box-like construction, the sides outline-cut to form simple arms. Most of the cheaper furniture in south Germany was made of pine, and it seems probable that it was also used for these functional items which were arranged in a row along the walls of the nursery or lying-in room. In the same period, side chairs of slat construction were used in the kitchens, so that infants who could walk could be fed in their own miniature seats.

Few early pine children's chairs have survived, as they were often too crudely made to be treasured, but some concept of their variety of design can be gained from the miniatures that are found in 17th- and 18th-century cabinet houses. In the Stromer House, in Nuremberg, Germany, a roughly constructed box-like baby chair is found in the nursery. Such chairs, with a tray across the arms for holding plates of food or toys, were common in peasant homes throughout Europe until the end of the 19th century; some, like the early Nuremberg example, had their own floor in order to keep the child's feet off the damp or cold ground.

Similar high-backed chairs, made from simple, shaped sections of plank, were made more comfortable by the addition of padding. One design that is particularly Dutch is a chair with a counter-like front which completely enclosed the child: a wise idea if the chair was to be used in a busy kitchen. Such chairs were, inevitably, quite heavy, so wheels were sometimes fitted. To amuse the child, a bell was hung from a metal bar at the front, a tradition that developed into the rows of large coloured wooden beads found on Victorian and Edwardian children's chairs.

Almost any old child's chair is collectable, as the small size holds immediate appeal for many people. Because the country versions were so strongly made, they are suitable for nursery use today, although it has to be admitted that the majority are now used as decoration. They fit well into almost any room and are small enough to be placed on a half-landing or in a narrow alcove that would not hold any adult-sized pieces. Many of the high-backed plank types were roughly put together at home by fathers and can present a deceptively early appearance. A few have a round hole cut in the seat for the child's chamber pot; some have a plain tray, and others rockers. In Continental Europe and the United States, many were originally flower-painted, but those of British origin are plain-painted or of natural wood.

A few high chairs (which raised the child to the level of an adult table top) were made by the plank-type method, but these are much rarer than the low versions, presumably because they were heavy to move and sometimes unstable. Lighter, slat-type designs were much more practical, as were the Victorian versions with dowel-turning which often incorporate several different woods. Very occasionally, a panelled or carved pine high chair is found but, in general, such workmanship was confined to the more expensive hardwoods.

Because of the interest in folk crafts that blossomed in the 1880s, a large number of miniature and children's chairs were made in antique styles. Craftsmen in tourist areas created charming and well-made copies of regional designs and would add the child's name and date in paint. In the United States, small suites of a sofa and two chairs were made in this manner and are particularly collectable if their family history is known. Smaller doll sizes were also made, and because of the widespread fascination with miniature furniture, these command higher prices. This interest in all types of child-size and miniature furniture has encouraged the manufacture of fakes and reproductions, and care has to be taken when purchasing expensive pieces. Some of the old reproductions made in the Edwardian period have now gained a place of their own among antique furniture, as they were well-made and skilfully painted. In the early 20th century, it was fashionable to arrange a collection of such chairs along a hall or in the drawing room, so they have been considered respectable antiques for some time.

Few modern craftsmen make complex pine children's chairs, although the simple plank types are reproduced in some number and are sold by most specialist pine dealers. They are so strong that they are ideal for nursery use, but the majority are used for decoration.

OPPOSITE A *contemporary pine settee based on the simple line associated with the German Beidermeir period.*

ABOVE A *variety of bedroom and kitchen chairs can be found in the workrooms of most country-pine dealers. The commode chair has a shaped apron to conceal the chamber pot.*

TABLES

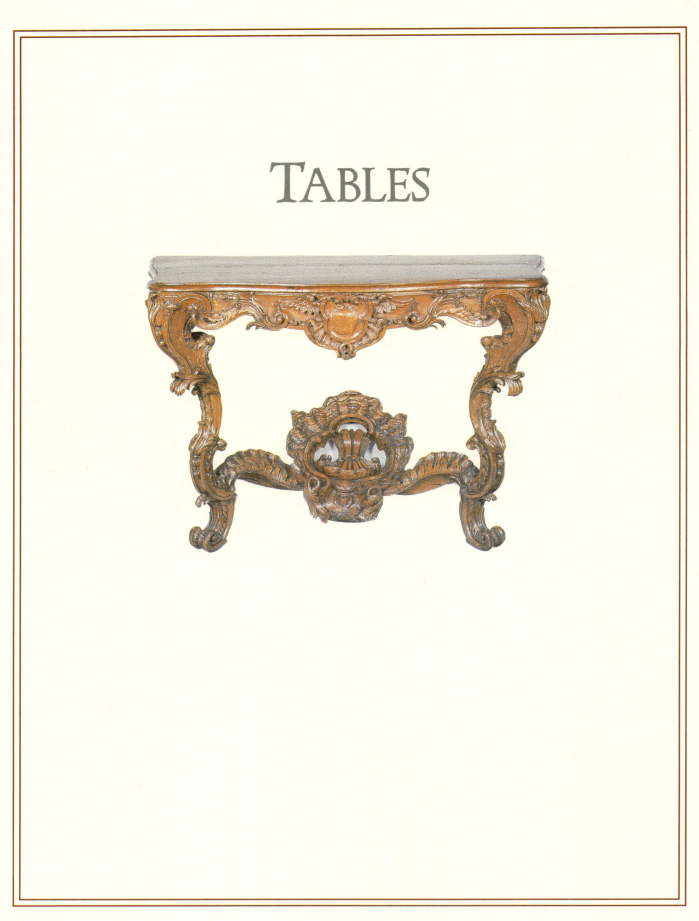

IN COUNTRY HOUSES on both sides of the Atlantic, the kitchen table was the centre of the home and all household activity: on its well-scrubbed surface pastry was rolled, rabbits and fish cleaned, brass and copper polished, and, in the evenings, it was covered with a plush or chenille cloth before books and needlework were brought out and the oil lamps lit. It was not unknown for an unexpected visitor to sleep on the table, or for it to be used for laying out a corpse! Little wonder that its construction was so solid.

Banished from the built-in, streamlined cooking areas of the 1960s and 1970s, the old kitchen giant was replaced with tiled 'eating surfaces' or fragile, Formica-covered flaps, which were not allowed to intrude on the carefully planned design. Today, as built-in furniture becomes less fashionable, the central table has reappeared in traditional kitchens, to become a meeting place for the whole family. The demand for tables of this type is so great that some manufacturers now specialize in country styles, producing scaled-down versions for small rooms.

Early British kitchen tables were straight-legged with a plain frieze and stretchers. They were usually the work of local carpenters, who did the final assembly of the table in the house. An original example of this type of pine table would now be quite expensive, as comparatively few have survived,

OPPOSITE *Pine at its most sophisticated is seen in this Louis XV console table. It is one of a pair, both with marble tops. The frieze has a central heart-shaped cabouchon, flanked by wings and scrolled foliage; mid-18th century.*

ABOVE *The old kitchen at Clandon Park in Surrey, England built in the early 1730s. The long, scrubbed table has a pot board for stacking crockery and utensils and several large drawers. Such tables were an essential feature of all large British houses in the 18th and 19th centuries.*

RIGHT *The kitchen at Canons Ashby House in Daventry, Northamptonshire, England. The 16th-century manor house was altered in the 17th century but has remained largely unchanged since 1710. The side table with shelves above it on the wall illustrate how the dresser form developed. The table has unusual apron sides and a pot board. Duckboards near sinks were sometimes made of pine and helped keep the maids' feet dry, as kitchen floors often ran with water.*

ABOVE *A 17th-century American trestle table with the top made from three pine planks. It has black-painted legs joined by a shaped central stretcher. It was made in New York State.*

ABOVE RIGHT *A nicely proportioned small, blue-painted chamber table made in Finland in the 19th century. It has turned legs joined by plain stretchers.*

and could be used today in combination with 18th-century chairs to give a dining room the relaxed country ambience that is often chosen in preference to formal dark oak or mahogany.

The typical turned-leg kitchen table became popular in the early 19th century and continued to be produced until the 1930s. As the basic structure was so rigid, stretchers were unnecessary. Smaller tables have a single drawer set into the frieze, but those intended for the large basement kitchens of town houses can have as many as four, fitted with turned wood or white earthenware handles.

It was once almost impossible to sell large tables of this type, but demand is now so great that reproductions are used to augment the supply. The tops of Victorian examples are sometimes badly stained or scorched and it is not uncommon to find new tops attached to an old base. Traditional kitchen tables made by modern craftsmen are not cheap, as their construction demands good quality timber to give the solid look that is so essential.

The long tables that were used in the kitchens of grand houses were completely different in construction to the all-purpose examples found in smaller homes. A number have survived, as they were constructed in the kitchens and are impossible to remove in one piece. They have a deep frieze which would have made them very uncomfortable to sit at, as well as stretchers which would have added to the discomfort. In effect, such tables were the equivalent of the island units in modern kitchens. There was frequently a rack that ran the length of the table and was supported by the stretchers; this was used for the storage of metal pans, cooking pots and almost anything that could not be eaten by mice or domestic pets.

The many drawers fitted around the table contained kitchen tools, and on the table top stood another rack-like structure that held the more fragile crockery and glass; in this way, servants working around the table were provided with a vast assortment of equipment in one central area.

In Great Britain and the United States, this type of table was not made in smaller sizes but was a design used exclusively in important houses or institutions. They are seen in small domestic sizes in Germany, however, where, packed with copper and brass, they formed a decorative centrepiece for the kitchen. Narrower versions were commonly used for extra storage and preparation space around the sides of the room. Instead of the racks seen under most British examples, the German models have plain wooden platforms. Tall versions with two shelves were especially effective when packed with display china, and resemble the oak buffets of an earlier period.

In German merchant houses of the 16th and 17th centuries, there was a large living room where food was prepared and eaten. In the centre of such rooms stood a big pine-topped table for dining, with a smaller version for ironing or sewing which was left without a cloth. Tables of all shapes and sizes were arranged in bedrooms and reception areas and were used for card playing, toilette, sewing, eating and drinking. Their basic construction was simple and cheap, as the whole table was covered with a cloth or table carpet

LEFT *An exceptionally well made central table in the kitchens of Castle Drogo in Devon. The castle was built between 1910 and 1930 and was designed by Edwin Lutyens (1869-1944). The kitchen was furnished in traditional British style with a built in dresser and large preparation table.*

that cost many times more than the piece of furniture it covered. Folding tables, which hung from the walls, were another feature of German houses until the 18th century, although even after this date they were sometimes found in small kitchens. The tradition of the pine flap table was continued in several countries; in Ireland, for instance, they are recorded in Ulster, where board tables are also seen. The most ancient form of table, the board table was simply a section of wood that could be placed across the lap, like a tray. They were scrubbed and hung on the walls between meals.

German peasant furniture makers constructed tables of simple flat shapes that were not only easy to cut, but also provided good surfaces for painted

BELOW *The kitchen at Erddig, near Wrexham in Clwyd, Wales – a mainly 17th-century house with 18th-century additions. The kitchen has a large butcher's block and a heavy table with unusually deep drawers at the end.*

decoration. Various pine trestle designs were common, some with a knee-level stretcher linking the side supports. Sometimes additional stretchers at foot level gave added strength. Four or five planks joined by a crosspiece formed the high back of primitive benches, which converted into dining tables when the backs were pegged down to the arms. Narrow table-cupboards, common to many European and American country homes, were arranged around the sides of the kitchen. The presence of stretchers at foot level, even when the construction of a table is so rigid that they scarcely seem necessary, is a feature of German peasant work found on both turned and straight-legged pieces.

Swedish country furniture, like that of other European cultures, is characterized by the need to economize with space. The ancient tradition of a pine board placed across the knees developed into plank tables which were supported by blocks of wood or, in the medieval period, simple stools. When the meal was finished the table top was hung from heavy iron rings on the wall. Gradually, the trestle table became common, as this too could be taken apart easily when extra space was needed.

Occasionally, a date was carved or painted on the stretchers of these Northern European tables, but otherwise they are difficult to attribute to a precise period as the designs changed so little. One interesting and space-saving Swedish type that appears to have been introduced in the 17th century consisted of a table on reeded legs which stood on a shallow, box-like base where utensils were stored, and the table frieze contained a further drawer for linen. Table chairs are another characteristic Swedish design, although they must have been extremely uncomfortable. A single strut of wood, painted or outline-cut, formed the very narrow back rest. When a small table was required, this back strut was turned down to form a fourth leg and the chair seat unfolded.

Because early country furniture in Great Britain was so crudely made, it has rarely survived. The earliest recorded mention is of a 15-ft (4.5-m) trestle-type table that was included in a 1542 inventory of the contents of the 'Great Dynyng Chamber' at The Vyne, a house in Hampshire, England. At this time, tables of pine and deal seem to have been quite acceptable in grand houses, and another was used in the dining room of Howard House in Kent, England. Billiard tables were frequently made of oak and pine in the 16th century, although, again, surviving examples are extremely rare.

Trestle tables were not only used for eating but also in bedrooms, where they were covered with a cloth. Folding-top tables appeared in many areas of the home, used for card playing and taking light meals. Deal folding tables, as well as various small cupboard types, were known in Tudor homes and were very much the equivalent of occasional tables. Small tables with flaps are usually referred to as breakfast tables, although the country versions were more frequently used for writing or sewing. In the late 18th century, delicate versions were made in pine by established cabinetmakers working for wealthy customers, but the wood was invariably japanned or painted. Examples with surfaces that were damaged beyond repair occasionally appear

ABOVE A Northern European gate-leg table, painted in light grey and dating to the late 18th century. It is thought to have been made in the town of Nora in Vastmanland in Sweden.

in the stock of pine dealers and are stripped and polished to give some idea of the quality that was possible when town makers used the wood.

The finest work in pine was designed by artist-decorators such as William Kent (1685-1748), who made great use of it for the carcasses of tables. Marble-topped tables with gilded frames are often carved in great detail, as are the side and pier tables designed by Robert Adam (1728-92). Oak and pine, veneered with rosewood, was used for a number of tables and desks, and Adam-style pieces are occasionally found with the veneer removed to reveal the base wood. This treatment used to be resorted to when the veneer was in too bad a state to be restored and has meant that some items which otherwise would not have survived have been preserved, even if they are in a different idiom.

Pedestals, pier tables and delicate girandoles, as well as items such as hall seats, were designed by Adam for construction in pine. These were normally gilded, but some pieces, such as the hall seats, were painted white. Copies of this classical British furniture were made by many cabinetmakers, especially in the United States, and in consequence a number of high quality pieces of this type appear on the market among the most expensive of pine items. The United States saw a much greater production of such designs in pine which were not intended to be covered with veneer or paint, and these now give a most elegant look to houses decorated in the ever-popular Federal style of the first half of the 19th century.

In the gardens of elegant Federal-style houses, green-painted round pine tables were popular. These were derived from the plank-type constructions that were used for European peasant furniture and show German and Scandinavian influences. In Great Britain, three-legged round tables, popularly known as cricket tables, were found in almost every 18th- and 19th-century

FAR LEFT *Traditional furniture designs from several periods are sometimes combined by modern craftsmen to create pine dining-room suites. Such furnishings can be integrated into old or new houses.*

LEFT *A small Victorian three-legged table with turned legs. This type was very common in Britain and was used mainly in bedrooms. They were often painted or stained. Today they can be used in any part of the house and make good lamp tables.*

A B O V E *The simple lines of this writing table with two drawers in the frieze makes it ideal for use in a hall or study. This example, seen in an auction room, is typical of the furniture that can be found in regular fortnightly sales.*

home. They were sometimes extremely plain, with undecorated legs and stretchers, and were made of a number of different woods. Often associated with the three stumps used in the game of cricket, it is now thought that the term 'cricket table' was derived from a cracket, which is a three-legged stool in the north of England. In early 17th-century examples of the cricket table, the stretchers were situated at the base of the legs, but by the mid 18th century, they had been moved to halfway up so that a shelf could be fitted. Early pine versions are very rare, but the vast numbers that were constructed in the 19th century did use pine. It is these pine and deal cricket tables that are often found today, frequently misattributed to an earlier period.

The design of a cricket table was eminently practical, as the tables stood securely on uneven floors and were ideal for kitchen or garden use. Crudely made pine versions were supplied by the hundreds in the 1920s and 1930s for hotel and pub gardens, and for tea rooms. Some of the garden tables look convincingly ancient, as they were left out in all weathers. Reproduction versions are now produced for use in kitchens or as the central tables for small dining rooms, while very small examples are useful for the bedside or for occasional use in a sitting room.

Small round bedroom tables, with a plain frieze linking the turned legs, were almost invariably made of pine and were found in the houses of both rich and poor until World War II. Originally most of these cheap tables were painted, as they were mainly used in less important bedrooms, but they are now stripped and take on a new lease of life in chintz-hung rooms. As furniture with turned legs is sometimes found to have been constructed of different woods, it is advisable to purchase a table that is stripped already, otherwise hours of patient work can end in disappointment when particularly ill-matched sections are revealed.

As these tables were so common, there is not much difference in price between old and reproduction versions. Many modern craftsmen will make tables of this type to the exact size required, so that a matched pair can be used in a bedroom or a group can act as lamp and occasional tables in the drawing room. As pine is no longer considered only a kitchen wood, some superb dining-room pieces are being made; thus, a complete setting could be used to give a Federal effect, particularly successful when combined with pine-panelled walls.

Large craftsman-made tables and sideboards compare well in price with the mass-produced furniture of today, and are a much better investment; the pieces made by known workshops will become the antiques of the future.

BELOW *The traditional pot-board dresser form, updated to create a side-table for a modern dining room. The functionalism of the original concept is maintained and the wood is shown to advantage.*

CUPBOARDS

EMPTY CUPBOARDS not only revealed poverty but suggested that the mistress of the house was a poor organizer, who lacked the ability to manage family affairs. Such a situation spelled disaster in any rural environment, as the comfort of the household depended on a woman's skill in making the most of anything that came her way. Women in all European peasant cultures carefully stored non-perishable foods, crockery and good quality linen so that the family had some assets to fall back on in times of difficulty.

Cupboards and chests are the simplest forms of storage furniture for a carpenter to construct, and in some of the poorest Russian peasant interiors, complete rooms were lined with robust lockers of different sizes that were made attractive by their lively painted decoration. In larger houses, pine storage furniture is particularly associated with the kitchens and servants' quarters, where many cupboards were built-in. In the Netherlands and Germany, some storage fitments were glazed, so that the well-arranged crockery and plate could be admired.

In this affluent age, few storecupboards are so beautifully arranged that they can be left open: instead, we choose designs that conceal the mass of untidy equipment inherent to a throw-away society. Although fitted pine kitchens can give a rural atmosphere when decorated with the right accessories, they are essentially designed to conceal as many items as possible in the smallest space. Such kitchens have created a great revival in pine furniture making, and are the most significant development in the use of the wood in the 20th century, revealing a curious mixture of the practical and romantic. While most contemporary designs are streamlined, others incorporate some of the more interesting features of country furniture, such as spindle-turning, small spice drawers and marble working surfaces. Despite all these embellishments, however, the basis of the design has to be the series of cupboard base units that provide the main storage area.

Pine suits kitchen furniture particularly well, and good effects can be achieved by using inexpensive cupboards. One simple method of establishing order in a small kitchen is to hide away all the white mechanical monsters – fridges, washing machines and microwave ovens – behind ceiling-to-floor pine doors that can be constructed locally and transform the kitchen at relatively low cost.

Ornate cupboards for kitchens and bedrooms are often based on original French designs for the massive armoires (wardrobes) that were the pride of every bourgeois and peasant family. The finest were made by trade guild members or master joiners in urban workshops. The armoires, of chestnut, fruitwood, walnut or pine, were made in large numbers in all parts of France for peasant homes, in general much better furnished than their equivalent in Germany or Great Britain. Although some pieces exhibit regional characteristics, the majority of makers relied on the design books, templates and profile curves that were generally available. Pieces in the traditional Louis XV style, lavishly decorated with carving, continue to be made up to the present

OPPOSITE A *small wall cabinet that was made in Finland and dated 1788. It has two arched doors that open to reveal three shelves. It is flower painted and retains the original fittings.*

ABOVE A *very fine, early 18th-century painted American corner cupboard with a glazed upper door and reeded columns. The lower doors have fielded panels and the original 'H' hinges.*

day, although modern versions, unless made as exact reproductions, are much smaller. Most of the pine examples are less complex than the fine pieces in chestnut and occasionally have glazed doors which look less impressive than panelling.

Armoires are effective in almost any environment: on a half-landing, in the dining room, or, because of their good storage space, in bedrooms. Good antique examples have well-fitted interiors, although the divisions were not infrequently removed to allow more hanging space. Versions without evidence of the removal of original dividers should be examined carefully, as the cupboard might have been recently assembled from a pair of old doors combined with a new back and sides. As armoires were sometimes built into houses, there are a number of doors available and they obviously command a much higher price if they are made up into a piece of furniture. There is nothing essentially wrong with this practice, but the purchaser should be aware of the adaptation.

The most ancient cupboards were made for the storage of food and were built into walls for coolness. Other early cupboards were positioned in chimney walls to keep the salt or tinder-box dry. Domestic pine examples are recorded in Great Britain from the 15th century, when a 'spruce hutch' was mentioned in a will. These spruce cupboards were used for food, clothes and valuable hangings and were exported from the Baltic region to several countries. The terms 'press', 'hutch' and 'aumbrey' were all used to describe cupboard-type structures found in both wealthy establishments and poorer homes in the Elizabethan period.

A cupboard intended for the storage of food can always be recognized, as ventilation was essential. This necessity led to a wide range of decorative as well as practical solutions, and the finest examples have forms of baluster in-filling instead of panels. Cheese cupboards were constructed in a similar way until the late 19th century, those with delicate turned spindles being much more desirable than the coarse rural versions with plain slats. Other food cupboards have the door panels or planks pierced with neatly drilled holes. These are sometimes extended over a complete door and arranged in complex patterns, although more frequently there are a few lines of regular sized holes. Pierced tin panels, treated decoratively, are found on some American versions, and another unusual method of ventilation was to fit panels of wickerwork to the sides of a plank cupboard (possibly a cheap local substitute for wire mesh).

The meat safes used in the kitchen areas of large houses would generally have been well-made by an estate carpenter, but those found in cottages were frequently home-assembled. In order to stop pilfering, locks were fitted and the key kept by the housekeeper. Until the mid 20th century, poorer households often kept their meat cool in summer in a padlocked safe outside the kitchen door, and there are still a number of these commercially made structures in circulation. They can look interesting when the mesh or pierced zinc is cleaned and the pine waxed, and can be useful in a modern kitchen for keeping insects off prepared dishes.

OPPOSITE *Cupboards intended for the storage of food can be recognized by the presence of ventilation holes. This Irish example, c.1860, has simple rails in the upper doors.*

ABOVE A *Swedish two-part cupboard with the top and bottom separated by an open shelf. It carries the date 1845 and has two carved lions on the top. Such heavily decorated pieces are superb examples of folk art but are now rarely found. This example came from the Ingelstorp Parish in Skåne.*

In Northern Europe, heavy Renaissance-style food cupboards with complex spindles and carved slats remained popular until the 19th century, when much lighter pine became common. In most well-equipped German kitchens, there were several cupboards of this type, including small, hanging versions, sometimes with a stencilled decoration on the doors. Everything from eggs to the household keys were neatly organized in such cupboards, which were constructed with delicacy and are now very collectable. Small pieces like these were sold by journeymen at the great fairs; today, Swiss or German housewives can buy reproductions in street markets and craft shops.

The most important piece of furniture in German houses was the traditional great cupboard, of which the finest examples were constructed in the Renaissance style, with the fronts divided into panels. The best were made of walnut or fruitwood, but pine versions are also common. As they were so massive, they stood in a vestibule or on a broad landing, and were frequently made in two sections, so they could be moved. The painted examples were the glory of south Germany, with biblical scenes, figures in national dress, buildings, flowers and birds all represented in ravishing colours.

Artists who paint in the traditional manner are still able to decorate a pine cupboard to family-heirloom standard, and their work is seen in expensive folk-art shops in Munich or Berchtesgaden. Similar cupboards were used in the Netherlands and were introduced by Dutch craftsmen to the United States where they were known as 'Kas' (an adaptation of 'Kast', meaning cupboard). Made in New York and New Jersey until 1900, they were often plain, but, because of the German influence, there were some painted versions, occasionally incorporating the initials and dates of the original owners.

Such splendid cabinets are now costly, but there are many inexpensive pieces of Continental pine that are quite affordable. German-style washstand cupboards can be used to create a focal point in a bedroom or bathroom, as many late examples are curiously reminiscent of earlier designs. These tall structures were composed of a top cupboard covering a cistern, a hand basin and a further compartment for toilet items beneath. Late Northern European washstands are much lighter than their British and American counterparts, often comprising a plain wooden table with turned legs and a shelf beneath for water jugs and the slop bucket. English washstands are in the nature of cupboards on legs and are much more impressive, with tiled backs and marble surfaces. These are now among the most popular items in stripped pine and are such fast sellers that they are manufactured for the antique trade, as demand has far exceeded supply. They are adaptable items, and can be used instead of a cabinet in a bathroom or for storage in a bedroom. They occasionally appear in kitchens, as the marble tops make ideal pastry and preparation surfaces. Despite their popularity, washstands are still relatively inexpensive, and there is a wide selection of designs. Look for examples with their original handles, which were cast-iron or bronzed – but rarely brass – and with old tiles. Unfortunately, these later often cracked as the washstand was subjected to heavy daily use, and have been replaced with modern designs which spoil the effect.

ABOVE *An exceptionally fine cupboard with painted drapery, a typical form of decoration in Jamtland, Sweden. It has marble effect decoration as well as traditional flower patterns and is dated 1805.*

OPPOSITE *A modern pine wardrobe made in Britain in late 19th-century style with two drawers in the lower section and hanging space above. In the 19th century such wardrobes were usually stained or painted but look attractive in natural wood.*

BELOW *An unusually well made American food safe with a shaped apron, dating from the 18th century. Food safes of a more rustic type were often kept out of doors. The sides can be of pierced metal, wire mesh or wickerwork.*

RIGHT *An effective modern interpretation of a food cupboard with pierced work doors. This piece with its shaped lower doors and deep cornice is better finished than most antique examples and is intended for use in a dining room.*

OPPOSITE *Large painted cupboards of this type were used in most Northern European countries for the storage of vast quantities of linen that exhibited the wealth of the family. This piece, from Alaveteli in Finland dates to the late 18th century and is painted with the skill of the professional decorator.*

Originally, the washstand formed part of a complete bedroom suite, which could have had as many as eight pieces. Deal and pine suites were mass-produced for the working-class market after 1875, and were grained, stained or painted. Few have survived complete, so that a well-stripped and polished setting would be relatively expensive today, despite its original low price. The better wardrobes contain shelves, trays, hanging spaces and compartments for the gloves, hats and collars that were necessary for Victorian respectability. Some of these wardrobes are more attractive inside than out, and can provide a decorative focal point if filled with antique clothes or patterned textiles, and the doors left open.

It is almost impossible to acquire pre-18th-century clothes presses, as those made of pine were usually built-in and painted to match the wainscot. In general, clothes cupboards became much smaller during the Georgian period (1714-1830), when they were more likely to be moved from place to place. Satinwood and mahogany were used by the leading cabinetmakers, leaving pine for country craftsmen or where a painted finish was acceptable. When Thomas Chippendale (1718-79) designed a wardrobe with glazed doors for the actor David Garrick, painted pine was used for the elegant piece,

OPPOSITE *A small cabinet with the date 1761 made in Seinäjoki in Finland. It has chip carving in crude geometric shapes and slender panels to the sides of the splay front.*

ABOVE LEFT *A large Yorkshire housekeeper's cupboard with the well proportioned panels that indicate a structure that was originally expensive and intended for a large house.*

BELOW LEFT *Small hanging cupboards were often very brightly painted to provide a splash of colour in the dark interiors during the long winter months. This Swedish piece is from Dalarna and is dated 1783.*

RIGHT *A heavily constructed small cupboard from Kokkola in Finland, dating to the 18th century. The cornice has unusual decoration and the centre panel has stylized carving in similar designs to those seen on chairs.*

ABOVE *The good patination of a piece that has never been painted. This cupboard from Korpilahti in Finland was made in the 18th century and has an unusual pediment decorated with finials.*

which was surmounted by a carved urn. Similar wardrobes of deal with panelled doors were made in all parts of Great Britain and America, using cabinetmaking designs that changed very little until the mid 19th century and were revived early this century in the Edwardian period. Craftsmen now frequently use these Georgian designs as inspiration for office or living-room storage, as they can be fitted to hold electrical equipment, books or filing cabinets.

In Europe, the wardrobe was the province of the middle classes and only made its appearance in bourgeois country homes. In comparison, that user of little space, the corner cupboard, is found in all areas and remained a feature of country homes long after disappearing from fashionable interiors. British corner cupboards are especially associated with the reign of William & Mary (1689-1702), although they became most popular in the 18th century when they were japanned or painted, and sometimes stood on elegant stands. Unfortunately, some of the painted pieces were stripped in the 1970s, when lacquered furniture was not liked; these dainty items still come on the market and usually sell quickly, despite their lack of complete originality.

Fitted deal corner cupboards were often painted to match the panelling or wainscot and are stripped when they are removed from old buildings. As fashionable cupboards were intended for the display of china, the shelves were prettily shaped and the interiors painted in green, blue or pink. Sometimes wallpaper was used as a lining and can help to date a piece. In some instances, the doors were glazed so that the china was always on view. As elegant people began to buy special display cabinets, corner cupboards became country and provincial pieces, with very few design changes. Some are almost architectural, with classical split pediments, shaped shelves, reeded pillars and shell-shaped backs. As the interiors are so attractive, the outer doors were sometimes removed. This obviously affects value, so look for scars left by the original locks or fittings. If purchasing a top quality pine corner cupboard as an investment, look for 18th-century 'H' hinges, original lock plates, fielded panels, canted corners and a splendid pediment. Some fine pieces have fret panels, additional small drawers and even retain the interior paint. Any piece that exhibits several of these features is well worth buying, especially if the wood is nicely patinated.

European peasant versions are basic in construction and made for use as functional items rather than for display. Some are a combination of cupboards and drawers, others come apart in several sections. In Sweden, the top and lower sections are occasionally divided by a central shelf area, with galleries supported on pillars for the storage of plates. In the west of Sweden, some have dresser-like tops with several open shelves. The corner cupboards and other furnishings were often painted by itinerant decorators, although the finest work is that of known specialists. In Russia, painted decoration supplanted household carving, and in the late 19th century much of the furniture was finished in the towns because of the interest in traditional crafts.

Throughout the world, regional names are given to specific types of furniture, such as the American jelly cupboards or those used in Wales for salt. These terms are sometimes used in the antique trade to give importance to crudely made pieces of little real merit, although the added titles do make buying more fun.

Until a few years ago, the big linen cupboards that were a feature of country houses were almost unsaleable; now, popularly known as housekeepers' cupboards, they are enjoying a boom. The new fashion for free-standing kitchen furniture has fostered interest in them as they offer so much storage space and can be used for china as well as linen. Cheap examples, with plank fronts and primitive metal hinges, could have belonged equally well in an outhouse as in the housekeeper's room. At best, they are well-made, with fielded panels of different sizes and standing on a plinth or bun or bracket feet. A few have locks, especially those used in important houses, where very expensive linen was stored.

Shelves or sliding trays were fitted in the upper sections, with deep shelves in the base cupboards for thick blankets or pillows. Top and bottom cupboards were usually pegged together so they could be moved, but a large number were built-in. If a very large example does not come apart, it is as well to check for new backs and side pieces, and a price that reflects such an adaptation. Small linen cupboards were used in rural homes but were not made to a particular design, so they are difficult to differentiate from all-purpose storage areas. Housekeepers' cupboards are now especially associated with more important houses, where the checking of the laundry was a weekly ritual supervised by the mistress of the house.

BELOW A *modern china cupboard whose design is derived from 19th-century shop fittings. Such cabinets are extremely useful for the display of collector's items.*

DRESSERS
AND
SHELVES

J H ELDER DUNCAN, the author of *The House Beautiful*, published in 1909, commented that in modern kitchens, 'A dresser, some shelving, a cupboard or two and a rack for dish covers, are included as part of the fixtures.' All the householder needed to add for a well-furnished room was a fender, a deal table and a few chairs. No decorative additions were suggested for this area; very different to the attitude of contemporary interior decorators, who give more attention to the kitchen than the hall.

Edwardian kitchen fittings were made of painted deal and varied in quality from utilitarian plank structures to pieces with interesting outline-cutting and well-made cornices. The influence of the Arts & Crafts Movement on the late Victorian period had fostered a revival of interest in dressers as fashionable items for the dining room, and these were fitted with long hinges and decorated with painted or carved mottoes, and cut-work hearts and spades. Such pieces, influenced by the designs of Englishman Charles Lock Eastlake, were popular on both sides of the Atlantic and exhibited the revealed construction methods which he advocated; a style of furniture, however, dismissed by *The Cabinetmaker* magazine as 'butter-tub and carpenter's bench'.

The traditional dresser inspired other contemporary designers, and in 1902 Scotsman Charles Rennie Mackintosh created fitted dining rooms with dresser units set between cupboards, pointing the way to the modern kitchen. Frank Brangwyn also experimented with up-dated dresser designs, but favoured low back-racks with just one or two shelves. Other designers made dresser backs more interesting by arranging the shelves asymmetrically, which gave an Art Nouveau effect when combined with long hinges in the style, or by using glazed cupboards with stained-glass panels.

The splendid oak and elm dressers that formed the main focus of interest in large 18th-century farmhouses have long been accepted as fine antiques and were in such demand in the Edwardian period that they were often reproduced. Pine dressers, thought of as junk furniture until the 1960s, are now following the same path and have moved from kitchens to dining rooms. They too are now reproduced and there are also good quality modern interpretations. Even the Edwardian deal kitchen fittings that were torn out when modern kitchen units became fashionable have been adapted as free-standing pieces and moved up-market to smart dining rooms or country-look breakfast rooms.

Dressers are composed of a group of shelves, known as the rack, set above a wider base, both sections being made of matching wood. As some were very large, they usually came apart. They began as a flat board that was used in the kitchen for dressing food for the table. Pine versions are particularly associated with Wales where, hung with lustre jugs, they were the pride of every housewife, whether she lived in a rural cottage or an industrial terrace. At the back of the shelves were arranged the large serving platters and dinner plates that were only occasionally used, as the dresser was thought of as a showpiece for the display of the best china. Since there were large

ABOVE *The bucket bench was a feature of the Pennsylvanian kitchen. This version, c.1760, has nicely shaped sides but cheaper versions were very crude.*

OPPOSITE *Many pine dressers were originally oak grained. This 19th-century English piece has the original graining in imitation of light and dark oak. It also has the original plaster mouldings and handles.*

cupboards in the base, ordinary items in daily use could be hidden from sight. This use of a dresser as a display piece is common to all country and peasant cultures, although the tradition seems to have originated in the Netherlands, where the 'best kitchen' was used for a lavish display of the rarely-used brass, pewter and china that the woman brought to a marriage as part of her dowry.

A good 18th-century pine dresser with nice patination, detailed shaping to the sides of the rack and a pleasing frieze now commands a high price. As oak dressers have soared in value, pine versions have become very desirable and in the mainstream of antique furniture. The best examples are those with an inimitable patina, gained from years of use, which gives a soft, honey-coloured effect, very different to the naked varieties that have come straight from the stripping tank. The best investment pieces are those dating from before 1800 and made in the country house, rather than the small cottage type. While all pine dressers made before 1920 will prove to be safe purchases, it is the classic pieces that will one day command prices comparable to similar designs in oak or elm.

Victorian pot-board dressers, with an open platform at the base, are less common in pine. In examples of the pot-board type, the base supports are profile-cut, reeded or turned, while the shallow drawers set into the apron can have wooden or china knobs or brass drop handles. Some occupied a complete wall of a Georgian kitchen, and they were sometimes built to fit around a corner. Most examples that appear on the market date before 1800, although there are reproductions of the more elegant designs.

In the 19th century, dressers with a fully enclosed base, containing cupboards and drawers, became most common. Exceptionally fine examples exhibit some special detail, such as a row of small spice drawers or good brass fittings. The long shelves of the rack are sometimes interspersed with small cupboards, or even a clock, which adds greatly to the desirability of the piece. The attention given to the cornice is very important, as it is another indication of a fine quality item. A breakfront or some decorative addition such as carving, not often seen on pine, would add to the appeal, as would good shaping of the sides of the rack. All these features give a pine dresser that added spark which attracts the discerning buyer.

J C Loudon, in his influential *Encyclopedia of Cottage, Farm and Villa Architecture and Furniture*, published in 1833, decreed that dressers were an absolute essential in every kitchen, but especially in cottages where they had to perform the dual functions of dressers and sideboards. He illustrated several designs for built-in dressers: one with a pot-board and straight legs, another with two cupboards in the base, separated by open central shelves. In this design, the arched panels on the cupboard fronts were reflected in the cut-work arches on the sides of the rack. Basic architectural designs such as these were intended as fittings in new houses and were usually painted. As pattern books were in widespread use in the United States, similar designs were used, with each carpenter adding some regional or personal detail. In some models from Pennsylvania, a frame of fret-cutting surrounded the rack, giving the dressers a Northern European character.

OPPOSITE *Extensive plate racks above the kitchen sinks in Castle Drogo in Devon, England. Smaller versions were common and stood on the draining board. They are now frequently reproduced.*

ABOVE A *mid-19th-century British dresser with a 'dog kennel' front and a shaped frieze. The open section in the base was intended for the large soup tureen that was the centrepiece of a dinner service.*

Modern copies of all the traditional pine dresser designs are now available, although the quality varies between those that are roughly made to imitate cottage-stripped pine, to finely finished craftsman-made versions that hold their own in any setting. The term 'Welsh dresser' is used for any British-style models with cupboards in the base. These can have a line of drawers above the cupboards or a group set in the centre. Mock drawers were quite common in the 18th century and were used to maintain the symmetry of the piece that was so essential to the Georgians. The Welsh dresser is a useful storage piece because of the generous cupboard space, although it can be a little clumsy in the largest sizes. Occasionally a clock was incorporated in the centre of the rack; this type is now popularly known as a 'Yorkshire dresser', even though they were in fact made in several areas. The term 'Lancashire dresser' is used for designs that include a breakfront cupboard in the centre of the rack. They usually have a central base cupboard with drawers set on either side. Most contemporary craftsmen recreate pieces in these traditional styles, but some dressers are made from an amalgamation of the better or more interesting features from several regions or countries.

In the second half of the 19th century, dressers were completely associated with kitchens, and the side cupboards of the rack were frequently glazed, especially those made for the Welsh industrial areas where open coal fires created a lot of sooty dust. The complexity of the glazing bars now adds considerably to the value. By the end of the century, the top was entirely enclosed by glass doors – not as attractive for the antiques buyer of today but

much more sensible for the housewife, struggling to keep her best china free from dust. These late industrial cottage versions often have a space between the base cupboards, causing them to be known as dog kennel types. In fact, the space, sometimes decorated with spindles, was used for the massive soup tureen that was the central piece in any dinner service. In farmhouse kitchens, the crocks that were used for dairy produce or for making ginger beer were kept in the dog kennel section.

Even small, cheaply made dressers with plywood backs to the cupboards now sell quickly, as they have great charm and contribute to the period atmosphere of kitchens and dining rooms. The plywood is especially prone to infestation by woodworm and is usually replaced with pine cladding or planks. Some of the thicker plywood is not immediately obvious when covered with several layers of paint. A high price should not be paid for an unstripped dresser, since several different woods might have been used. In general, unstripped pieces are best left to antiques dealers, who can restore and repair at a much lower cost than the private individual.

Victorian dressers look especially effective when a colourful earthenware dinner service is set out on the shelves. As so many old patterns are now reproduced, the colour scheme of the room can be keyed to the dominant shade of the china, while a less organized look can be created by a collection of jugs and dishes from many sources. Odd pieces of china look good if they are united by a common colour: blue-and-white or green-and-white china is not difficult to find, and can give a rich and fascinating effect, especially if attributable items are selected.

Almost any piece of furniture with a plain board top that can be used for serving could be termed a dresser. In medieval castles, these table-like structures were draped with fabrics and used for the display of the most expensive family plate. Ornately carved Renaissance-style dressers in oak were very much the province of the nobility, but by the 17th century they were relegated to the kitchen. Throughout their history, dressers have moved from kitchen to dining room or hall as fashions in household decoration have changed. They were again briefly fashionable after 1650, when they were used in halls and parlours, but went back to the kitchens of elegant houses after 1750. Fortunately, they never went completely out of fashion in country districts and are often found in farmhouses.

Pine versions were made in greater numbers in Scotland and Ireland than in England, where there was more hardwood available. In Ireland, the native oak forests had largely been destroyed by 1750, so the majority of dressers were made of softwood. The antique trade tends to describe any badly made or primitive British dresser with outline-cut front supports as 'Irish', especially those made from very thick pine. Despite the unfortunate proportions of some of these pieces, they sell quickly because of the current affection for primitive furniture. Some versions have a thin batten fixed in front of the shelves so that the plates can be tilted forward, in the German style.

French country dressers were much more ornate than the British equivalent, as the people took greater pride in their household equipment. The

ABOVE *The dresser concept is freely adapted by the makers of kitchen fittings. This version is fitted with downlighters and incorporates a sink.*

dressers are characterized by a lavish use of turned spindles, groups of small cupboards, carving on doors and cornices, and shelves of different widths and sizes on a single rack. These highly decorative structures are known as *Buffets Vaisseliers* or *dressoirs*, and were originally used for the display of family silver at the great Christian feasts. By 1800, the *Buffet Vaisselier* had become a provincial item of furniture, the best examples originating in Normandy or Arles, the furniture-making centre of Provence. Some of the largest, standing 10 ft (3 m) high, originated in the Bas-Pyrénées area. Deep in the countryside, Louis XIII and Louis XV styles lingered on for many years, so that it is often very difficult to date some of these massive *dressoirs* accurately.

French peasants organized their lives much more carefully than the casual American and British country folk, practising birth control in order to avoid splitting family possessions and making sure that their children made advantageous marriages. Their furniture, which was heavy and well-made, reflects this sensible attitude to life. Good, ornamental dressers are now used mainly in dining rooms, because of their decorative quality.

German dressers and shelves are also more complex than those found in Great Britain and the United States, although the intrinsic quality is not as high as that seen in French homes. Before the 18th century, narrow dressers with a pot shelf and a few drawers in the base were common in kitchens and were similar to those found in Great Britain. Other early German dressers have cupboards in the deep lower section, then a row of small drawers for spice in a narrower area. The rack, with decorative outline-cutting to its sides, was narrower still, so that the complete dresser was made up of virtual steps. This affection for ornament is also seen in the curiously primitive shelves made in Hungary, with complex but naïve projections from the sides and the shelf fronts – structures that seem designed for a people with a real affection for curves, spikes and pierced ornament.

Hungarian hanging racks and shelves frequently contain a few spice drawers, but were mainly intended for the display of plates, which were held in position by a gallery of profile-cut pillars, separated by plain dowelled uprights. The makers seem to have concentrated on creating the most curious structures possible and there are racks and shelves of every shape. Some were made in triangular form, similar to those found in German houses, where they were used for the display of cups. Most of the small shelves and racks were painted, and the Hungarian woodworkers sold them at the seasonal fairs. Reproductions of these designs are seen today in many antiques markets, their primitive structure creating a look of great age. If purchased cheaply as copies, they can give a lighthearted touch to a functional setting and are especially useful for the display of a small collection, such as egg cups or individual moulds.

Because of the lack of space in most European kitchens, a variety of hanging shelves and racks were made, so that every available section of wall could be used. The shelves of dressers and wall racks have notches cut along the fronts for spoons. Some dressers have a shelf for soup bowls beneath the spoon rack; silver spoons were treasured in German homes, and many racks

ABOVE A *traditional early 19th-century-style English dresser with shaped side supports and the original wooden knobs. These large pieces are now mainly used in dining rooms.*

RIGHT In this kitchen, a large 19th-century English dresser is used together with a hanging plate rack and a pine table. The room illustrates the current fashion for unfitted kitchens in which antique pine can be combined with interesting accessories.

were created especially for their display. Some are free-standing and were placed on a coffer or at the front of a dresser, while others were hung on the wall and are stepped. Spoon racks were used in Britain and the United States, but the designs are less complex: usually a double rack for the spoons and a box at the base, without a lid, for knives and forks.

The very large platters of pewter or earthenware that were used for serving meat were much too big for wall racks, and even for some dressers. Instead, they were stored in floor-standing racks that were constructed from lengths of dowel set in a pine framework. Some of the racks used in country-house kitchens were over 5 ft (1.5 m) high, but there were many smaller versions, some of which could be moved in front of the fire to warm or dry the plates. Similar hanging structures were fixed above the sink, so that the washed plates could drip-dry; today, these look charmingly old-fashioned in a rustic-style kitchen. The large racks are attractive when packed full of large platters and stood in a stone-flagged country-house kitchen. A few original plate racks still come on the market, but the majority are reproductions. As the basic construction is so simple, these look perfectly satisfactory if they are wanted for decorative effect rather than as a historical reconstruction.

Alcoves on either side of the chimney breast are the traditional position for arrangements of shelves. In old houses, plain pine shelving was fitted in kitchens with shaped front versions for the dining room or parlour. This is one of the simplest methods of creating a period effect inexpensively, as pine shelves can be fixed to decorative cast-iron brackets or to the wooden supports available from DIY and hardware stores. Pine shelves of this type can look attractive and practical in the kitchen if packed with glass storage jars or with one of the china cereal jar sets that characterized the Victorian American kitchen. They look equally good in a bathroom, if a complete wall is shelved for the display of glass containers or a collection of shaving mugs or hat-pin holders.

Dressers evolved from shelves that were fixed above a table or a coffer, and this remains one of the cheapest methods of creating the same effect. An old pine blanket box can be teamed up with a modern shelf unit, or a cast-iron rectangular garden table could have a row of shelves set on cast-iron brackets to give a lighthearted, ice-cream parlour effect in a conservatory or narrow hall. The built-in pine shelving and kitchen dressers that were a feature of Victorian houses can be reproduced in modern kitchens at encouragingly low cost, as the structure is invariably simple and assembled from sections of plank. All this white woodwork was scrubbed thoroughly each week, so that the deal kitchen tables and dresser tops in the best-run households gleamed white – treatment that was hardly good for the wood but ensured that the kitchen was spotlessly clean.

In some 17th-century German interiors, shelves that were set on ornamental carved brackets were fixed above the poultry coop where birds were fattened for the pot. Similar coops are seen in French peasant kitchens and in some 18th-century British interiors. These cage-like structures, with the fronts made from lengths of dowel or turned spindles, were incorporated into the

ABOVE A *sophisticated china display cupboard with glazed doors and reeded pillars suitable for use in a kitchen or drawing room.*

design of some Continental dressers. As they are now considered typical of the French peasant interior, dressers of this type are very desirable. Reproductions of cleverly antiqued pine are today made by several specialist firms, and these can give an atmosphere of a French fishing village to the darkest urban basement kitchen. Most decorators now use the coops for storing large platters, although earthenware or terracotta casseroles look even more impressive. The popularity of these chicken-coop dressers is another example of how a curious and amusing evocation of the past will sell well today, despite its impracticality.

LEFT An Irish country dresser with outline cutting to the plank legs. This example has an unusually ornate upper frieze. Most Irish country dressers are very simple.

ABOVE An exceptionally attractive set of display shelves dating to the late 18th century and made in England. It has a carved border around the arch and the shelves are well shaped.

CHESTS OF DRAWERS

ORDER WAS IMPORTANT in the well-run country home, and its mistress needed to control every aspect of daily life. Servants were notoriously unreliable and had to be protected from temptation, so linen and expensive foods needed constant checking and careful storage. To assist this process of supervision and organization there was an ever-increasing production of chests of drawers and storage furniture for kitchens, domestic areas and bedrooms, pieces that are as useful today as when they were first made.

The design of chests of drawers reached its highest point in the 18th century. Spices and sugar, being very expensive, were stored in drawers in the housekeeper's room or kept under lock and key in the kitchen. The small spice drawers are among the most charming of all country pieces, especially when they still carry their original painted content titles. The finest of these structures can stand over 6 ft (1.8 m) high and are fitted with drawers in many sizes. Some have large doors that can be locked but others, whose individual

OPPOSITE *An unusual late 18th-century chest of drawers with an exceptionally shallow bureau top, standing on bracket feet.*

LEFT *Pine chests of drawers of this type were used in most bedrooms in 19th-century Britain. With a looking glass on top, they served as a dressing table. They are again popular, as they provide so much storage space.*

drawers contained the more expensive spices, have fasteners. Miniature versions were made in large numbers for cottages, where they could be hung on the wall or stood on a chest or bench. Contemporary craftsmen make these attractive items for sale at shows and gift shops, and there can be few kitchens too small to accommodate a miniature of this type.

In the domestic store rooms of country houses, crudely made chests of drawers were used for items such as sugar. Sugar cones were large and required deep drawers with smaller ones above for the broken sections that were later ground for use. Currants and raisins were also consumed in quantity, and these were stored in drawers situated in a cool part of the kitchen or pantry. Furniture used for special storage of this type was simply made, often by the estate carpenter or a local woodworker. Despite their rough construction, any examples that carry labels or have some positive indication of their original use are of interest.

The 'mule chest', with drawers in the lower section, was probably the first stage in the evolution of the chest of drawers. Much greater skill was needed for this type of construction, so the item is seen less in the more primitive interiors, such as those in parts of Russia and Hungary. Variations on the mule chest have continued through the centuries, despite the impractical lifting top, but the greatest production in pine was in the United States, where they are termed 'blanket chests'. At the other extreme are the highly sophisticated japanned examples which were made by city cabinetmakers and exhibit the full potential of pine as a furniture-making material.

Country-style mule chests stand on bracket feet, which are the simplest to construct, although a few examples have bun feet. The japanned versions stand on slender cabriole legs that are part of a frame from which the chest can be lifted. Pine of this quality would never be stripped today, but specimens that received this treatment in the past occasionally come on to the market.

In the United States, easily transportable pieces like chests of drawers were ideal for the life-style of the early settlers. Pilgrim furniture was originally very heavy as it was made of oak, but pine soon became the most common wood, since it was easy to obtain and very much lighter in weight. Despite this use of softwood, many of the old oak designs were repeated and somewhat Renaissance-style pine chests were constructed. The blanket chest is the most typically American country piece and was made in a number of different styles, some of which reveal strong European influences. A few have a shallow, lidded section over two rows of drawers, while other designs have a wide central drawer with narrower drawers at the sides. The majority stand on legs or a deep plinth, allowing the contents to be lifted well above the ground away from damp and insects.

American blanket chests and chests of drawers were frequently painted to conceal the plainness of the wood used. This painting, in European peasant style, was usually confined to the drawer fronts, but in a few eye-catching examples, the whole piece was decorated. Another peculiarly American decorative technique, seen especially on simple plank-type chests of drawers,

ABOVE A 19th-century Swedish chest of drawers with a top that is painted in imitation of marble. The sides are painted in imitation of veneer, achieved using pigment diluted with beer. From Dalarna in Sweden.

OPPOSITE Pine is shown to best advantage in simple settings. Cottage doors of this type look especially good when stripped and waxed.

is the compass-drawn scratch and gouge carving. Stylized flowers are set in arches and circles, which transformed the plainest item of furniture into a lively decorative piece for a bedroom or living room. Vinegar-graining, marbling and stencilling are all techniques that were used to enliven carpenter-made furniture. Antique chests of this type are now very expensive because of Americans' affection for folk art, but are excellent investment items.

In the late Victorian period, the general interest in antiques and folk art encouraged the manufacture of many pieces in this idiom, and there is at present considerable production of old-style furnishings with painted and stencilled decoration. Most American country-craft shops have a wide selection of painted chests, and for a small extra fee, the new owner's name can be added in true settler style.

The term 'cottage furniture' is used in the United States to describe mass-produced 19th-century pieces that were made of softwood and flat-painted. The furniture was made more attractive by the addition of painted or, more usually, transfer-printed flower decoration. A characteristic of the chests of drawers in the style are the split spindles that were applied to the drawer fronts, a technique that originated in Germany. Furniture of this type, especially suited to small bedrooms, is also known as 'Jenny Lind' style, after the famous singer.

American country chests of drawers, made by local craftsmen, are often a mixture of tastes and styles; carved strapwork, spindles, low-relief carving, painting and gouge decoration are all combined to give a rich, almost Renaissance, effect. In New England, some chests of drawers have painted scenes on the front, and there are many curious forms that do not fall into any decorative mainstream – a projecting top drawer supported by pillars, for example. Most of these structures have wooden handles, presumably because the more sophisticated fittings were hard to obtain in remote areas.

OPPOSITE *A reproduction chest of drawers made in late 18th century style and fitted with drop handles. Pine will often look effective in a small space where almost any other type of furniture would seem out of place.*

LEFT *White ceramic handles are now popular on chests of drawers as they give a cottage-like effect. This chest is particularly appealing with the decoration on the drawer fronts.*

The custom of painting the name of the owner on chests of drawers has helped in the accurate dating of much American furniture, and the makers also seem to have marked their products more frequently than their European counterparts. The general interest in early furniture and folk art has meant that chests have been treasured in the original families, whereas in Britain it is only recently that country furniture has attracted attention.

Perhaps the most characteristically American of all country furniture is that made by the Shaker community. This religious sect made simple but well-constructed furniture both for its own use and for sale. The craftsmen worked to the strictures of the movement's founder, Mother Ann Lee, who advised craftsmen to 'Put your hands to work and your hearts to God'. Her philosophy guided her followers to construct furniture of such extreme simplicity that it points the way to the functionalism of the 20th century. The Shaker sect was founded in the late 18th century, and its followers made furniture for homes that were built according to the belief that order, clean lines, harmony and simplicity were necessary for a good spiritual life. Most of the furniture, from which all decoration such as mouldings and carving was banished, was made of pine. As 'beauty rests on utility', furniture that was embellished was thought to encourage pride and vanity, and hence was not to be sold or made by the believers.

Shaker furniture is now highly collectable, and the various designs of chests of drawers, for instance, give some idea of the variety of structures that could be created while working within this strict ethical code. One of the more typical chests is composed of three drawers of different depths in the lower section, with a line of small, narrow drawers above. Sometimes cupboards and drawers were combined in pieces of furniture on which the finish was always of the highest standard.

Fashionable finishes such as marbling and tortoiseshelling were banned from any good Shaker workshop, and were also despised by the English architect/designer/writer Charles Lock Eastlake, who exerted considerable influence on American furniture in the 1870s. He objected strongly to graining that was used on so much cheap deal furniture and described the practice as an objectionable and pretentious deceit. His chests with revealed construction were copied by most craftsmen who worked in the Arts & Crafts manner. Despite the intellectual popularity of his ideas, he had little impact on commercial furniture, and vast quantities of furniture continued to be created in grained pine. This involved laying on coats of white and yellow paint which, when dry, was washed over with a thin, transparent glaze. This was combed while still wet to give the characteristic streaked and grained effect. When dry, a further coat of varnish was added to give the shiny effect that was so hated by the followers of the Arts & Crafts Movement.

Other pine chest furniture, made especially for bedrooms, was sold plain with just a light varnish for protection. These suites were sometimes finished with a narrow line in green or blue or embellished with a few flowers. Curiously, Eastlake also disliked this plain pine, and suggested that it

ABOVE *An Edwardian dressing table awaiting restoration. Similar cheap furniture often formed part of a suite that would have been used in an artisan home.*

OPPOSITE *A chest of drawers with a low back-board standing on bracket feet. It has machine-carved decoration on the front and looks effective with a pine armchair in the hall of a town house.*

would be better covered with a plain stain. He felt that as deal was so soft and absorbent, it required some finishing coat for protection. As today's houses are so much cleaner because of the absence of coal fires in every room, this problem is of little concern to the interior decorator, who prefers pine in its untreated, natural condition.

Most pine chests of drawers tend to be of the plainer types that were intended for secondary bedrooms and for utilitarian storage. As general prosperity increased in the Victorian period, the amount of linen owned by each family became considerable and needed constant supervision. Every item was carefully marked and listed before it was placed in the correct drawer, where it could be located instantly. These big linen chests, sometimes kept in a special room, were supplied with brass label holders, similar to those used in draper's shops. Both these and the sensible wooden knobs are often replaced, which is a pity as the character of the furniture is so changed. Many of these utilitarian linen chests were painted in green or cream but are now usually stripped and waxed. They are ideal for use in kitchens or attic bedrooms, as their simplicity adds to the country atmosphere that is so fashionable today.

Highly decorative chests made of pine are very rare, and those that do come on the market are usually found to have been originally japanned or painted. A number of pleasing chests that stood on bun feet were made in the Chinoiserie taste of the late 18th and early 19th centuries and edged with bamboo. Originally these were painted pale green but more often than not were unfortunately stripped in the 1960s when such effects were not liked. This bamboo-decorated furniture was made for use in fashionable houses, hence its quality is good and the chests look effective in almost any setting.

As pine was used as a base for some veneers, chests that were badly damaged were sometimes stripped down to the pine. This type of piece was the work of cabinetmakers and of a high standard, so any such bureau or chest will be expensive. American craftsmen used pine much more frequently for high quality pieces, and there exist some superb examples of their work – all very expensive, especially when the maker's name is known.

Almost any unusual chest of drawers will attract keen interest, such as pieces with painted drawer fronts or bearing a family crest. A German chest of drawers with an integral child's bed with lattice doors at its top would be an obvious eye-catcher, and a fine piece to use as the focal point of an interior design. Tall, very narrow chests of drawers used originally to hold specimens of rocks and fossils are also good decorator's pieces, as they can be used for lamps or on either side of an entrance way. At the other extreme are the cheap drawers that were used in draper's and shoemaker's shops to store small items of stock; these now make ideal containers for papers, jewellery or handkerchiefs and are great favourites with children, providing a hiding place for dozens of treasures.

Almost every Edwardian bedroom was furnished with at least one large chest of drawers with sufficient storage space for many of the items of

ABOVE An English bureau dating to the late 18th century and shown in the open position with the flap supported on the slides. The interior is fitted with pigeon holes.

clothing that would now be hung in a closet or wardrobe. These chests of drawers are characterized by their large, turned-wood or china knobs and many have a secret compartment fitted in the top section of the side supports for the safe-keeping of private papers or a slim jewel case. With a small looking glass on top, these chests served as dressing tables in small bedrooms. They were considered too cumbersome by succeeding generations, and became almost unsaleable, but they are now enjoying a revival as they are ideal for creating a turn-of-the-century atmosphere.

Occasionally, chests of drawers were fitted with marble tops whose colour matched that of the washstand. In the United States, tops of this kind were used for sideboard-type structures, as the marble helped to keep food cool. Sometimes one section of a kitchen chest of drawers will have a marble insert, said to have been used as a surface for cutting cheese. Any piece with an unusual addition such as this attracts the interest of the antique trade, as well as interior decorators. Massive country pieces that combine deep drawers in the base with spacious top cupboards are liked, as they can be used to fill a complete wall and provide all the storage space that is required in a kitchen or dining room. Sometimes these vast structures have some unusual additions – such as a clock or a recessed centre cupboard, flanked by rows of small drawers – that take the pieces out of the basic range and provide features that the decorator can use as a central point in a furnishing scheme.

LEFT *A chest of drawers with turned feet and a high back board made in Britain in the late 19th century.*

BEDS
AND
CRADLES

THE BED'S POSITION in the Middle Ages as the most important and expensive item of furniture in the house has slowly been eroded until it has become one of its less interesting features: no longer status symbols but simple, functional supports for the body. The introduction of the low divan meant that heavy bed ends were unnecessary as support for the bed irons and they were replaced by unobtrusive padded headboards. The revival of interest in period styles has helped to encourage a new awareness of the design possibilities of an impressive bed, and there is keen competition at auctions for any good examples that appear.

OPPOSITE *This American folding bed was kept in the living room and was pulled down when needed. It comes from the Lee Room in the Summer House in Lee, New Hampshire, dated c.1740.*

LEFT *A pine cradle with painted ends, dated to 1813. It is decorated with the rose painting that was so popular in Northern Europe. The cradle comes from Lapua in Finland.*

Until the Edwardian period, the master bed remained the centre of the many rituals associated with birth, marriage, sickness and death, so the structure needed to be imposing. In the great medieval houses it was the drapery and hangings that were expensive rather than the bed itself, which, as it was completely concealed, could be quite simple. There were special hangings and covers for mourning, and for lying-in, a ceremony associated with the birth of a child when the mother remained in a splendidly equipped room to receive visitors.

In Northern Europe, where pine was readily available, it was used for the frames of the great State beds, sometimes in combination with other woods. Velvet- or brocade-covered testers and celures were combined with sumptuous tasselled and fringed curtains that draped the bed. As it became fashionable to expose the bedposts and celure, painted and gilded finishes were used to disguise softwood carvings and mouldings. Carved oak beds

were always the most expensive, and surviving examples are mainly made of this wood. Pine was used for less important rooms, and was found in the homes of common people.

One unusual but practical form that could well be revived for use in small flats was the 'press bed', designed to save space by fitting into a tall cupboard. Although this type was especially popular in peasant homes, it was also used in important houses, often for a servant sleeping in a master's or mistress's room. In some country districts, press beds continued to be made until the early 19th century and are found in cottage living and bedrooms.

The cupboard doors that conceal the bed during the day are hinged at the top and can be supported on poles to form a tester. The bed itself is also hinged and is lowered into position, and the hinged legs at the foot are then pulled down. Simpler versions without a tester were also made of pine: when Chippendale designed a painted pine press bed for the actor David Garrick in 1770, he went out of his way to conceal the true purpose of the structure by adding sham drawer fronts at the base of the doors, so that it appeared to be a conventional wardrobe.

Used from the earliest times, the simplest beds are those of low form, with a modest headboard that could be carved or assembled from turned sections. The mattresses, filled with feathers, straw or bracken, were supported on ropes and the bedclothes were held in position by bed staves at the sides. Truckle beds, low structures on wheels, were mainly used for servants and were often made of pine, as it was cheap.

Cupboard beds are found in all European countries and were used to conceal sleeping areas in farms and peasant homes particularly. Some of the finest appear in 17th-century Breton interiors in France, but good examples made of pine as well as the more favoured oak are found all over that country. These beds were used in any homes where living and sleeping were confined to one room, and are also sometimes seen in passages, where they provided extra accommodation for visitors' servants. In 18th-century French peasant interiors, the closed beds were lighter in structure and the early single doors were replaced by sliding double doors that were sometimes pierced or carved for additional ventilation. A few four-door cupboard beds have survived, whose beds were arranged above one another as with modern bunks, each layer having its own pair of doors.

Most French closed beds were supplied with a bench chest that acted as a step for climbing onto the high pile of mattresses. Spindles, seen on many pieces of peasant furniture, were used to decorate the doors of the cupboards. Reproductions of these beds are sometimes especially commissioned, but because of their size they do not appear in the stock of dealers; this is

LEFT *New Hampshire life between 1700 and 1730 is shown in the Lee Room at the American Museum in Bath. Here the folding bed (shown on page 96) is seen with the curtains that concealed it when not in use.*

ABOVE A *modern version of*
the sleigh beds that were
traditional in Northern Europe.
The sides of these beds always
remain neat as all the blankets
tuck in.

unlike French four-poster beds, also made precisely to fit between cupboards or into alcoves. The French peasant preferred a completely fitted effect that used space economically, and so only gradually did the bed become a separate piece of furniture. French decoration, even in country interiors, was much more sophisticated than that of Germany and Sweden. Plain, polished woods were favoured over the painted and carved ornament of the Northern European countries, where the decoration was often used to obscure inferior craftsmanship. Some well-designed French country furniture was stained with red 'oxblood', believed to prevent salt corrosion in areas near the sea.

The simplest form of bed is a pine plank fixed in the space between the ceiling and the stove, a warm but primitive arrangement that was found in numerous Russian peasant homes. Plank and settle beds are found in many European countries, but especially in Ireland, Wales and Scandinavia, where their use continued into the 19th century. As they were built into the room, few have survived, except in museum settings or well-preserved cottages.

In Hungary, the ornamental bed with its especially sewn and embroidered bedclothes was the most valuable and important item in the house. Like the State beds of the great houses, they were only used for special occasions and thought of as a symbol, for ornamental rather than functional use. When a girl married, the bed was displayed with all the beautifully stitched linen and covers she had made and then carried in noisy and ribald procession to the home of the groom. The ornamental bed became the decorative centrepiece of the new home and was so hung with embroidery that its pine framework was rarely seen.

Many of the plank-sided beds in vague Biedermeier style that are nowadays made for sale in pine shops are based on early Scandinavian designs. Unlike Hungary, where the structure of the best bed was rarely revealed, Swedish beds were made in such a way that the coverings were kept strictly within the pine framework, a framework which often resembled the sides of a sleigh. The earliest surviving examples date from the 16th century and stand on platform bases. The sleigh sides were extremely heavy, unlike some reproductions whose the sides are simply thin planks cut in the popular outline.

Renaissance-style Swedish beds of the late 17th century often combined a storage cupboard with a foot support for the tester. Because of the fear of vermin and damp, the sleeping platform was always set well above the floor, unlike the low box beds of Wales and Scotland which must have been infested with mice.

The most popular and most frequently reproduced Swedish design is the Gustavian bed, with a decorative sideboard that runs from head to foot. The Gustavian style is associated with the reign of King Gustave of Sweden (1790-1810), but lingered on for many years in rural districts. The high side was placed against the wall and was carved and painted, so that it resembled a settle rather than a bed. Some versions have an additional section that can be pulled forward to convert a single into a double bed. In all these Gustavian beds the mattresses are neatly fitted into box-like bases. Some of the designs

were reproduced around 1900 when interest in antique folk-type pieces was considerable; it is old reproductions from this late period which now appear most frequently on the market.

The anti-luxury laws and ordinances that governed Swedish furniture of the Gustavian period were similar in nature to those introduced by the American Shaker community, decreeing that woods and metals should not be used purely for ornament. Such ordinances resulted in far more severe styles than were common in countries such as Germany and Great Britain and encouraged a more sympathetic use of natural wood. Foreign artists and craftsmen who were brought into Sweden to supply the court with fashionable furniture did not influence country styles, and even the Empire style, known in Sweden as 'Karl Johan', hardly touched peasant interiors, which tend to mirror regional preferences.

As travel was so difficult in Sweden – except for a few summer months – fashions changed very little and the peasants held fast to the styles of their own provinces. Most of the furniture was made in the cold winter months when the makers were confined to their houses, with plenty of time to paint and carve the more important pieces. This practice was continued well

ABOVE Pine in traditional British style is brought up to date in this contemporary suite that could be used in town or country interiors.

into the 20th century, so that some country pine furniture looks much earlier than its actual date. As in Hungary, Swedish beds were piled high with mattresses, as family wealth was displayed by the number of featherbeds that were owned. Children and relatives often slept on simpler, built-in beds that were fitted around the walls of the main room. Some of the finest 18th-century beds were made by the craftsmen of the Angermanland province, while much of the painted work with rich carving came from Norrland.

In Germany, which was more cosmopolitan, furniture makers were influenced to a greater extent by foreign fashions, although pine beds, similar in construction to those of Sweden, were made. Some of the beds made for country houses are so impressive, with high headboards and detailed carving, that they resemble altars – especially those with centrepieces of painted religious scenes. As the bedclothes were tucked in at the sides, they presented a much neater appearance than British or American beds of the period, whose valances hung to the floor.

As part of her dowry, a German girl received a canopied bed and a cradle, both of which were painted and sometimes carved. The bed was the most important piece of furniture in a country house, closely succeeded by the guest bed. In some regions, these were painted by known artists who evolved their own recognizable styles, and whose work is now very desirable. Four-poster beds, first seen in the houses of nobility, were eventually copied for peasant homes; those made in the north are oak, but pine was generally used in the south. In Lower Germany, the tester was supported at the foot of the bed on two pillars, while the solid backboard held the top. By the end of the 18th century, four columns were more common, a style that spread across the country from Austria and the south.

Very high German beds sometimes concealed another bed on casters that could be pulled out when required. As in most European countries, cupboard beds, too, were common and were useful in giving some privacy in crowded living conditions; they were either carved or painted. They were piled high with pillows and mattresses, and a low chest was generally used as a step, although in Westphalia pine bed steps were provided.

Beds of a lighter style with turned decoration were in general use in Germany by the late 19th century, when design differences between European countries were not as great. Light structures resembling chaises longues were also common, especially in Switzerland and the Alpine regions of Germany, and these were placed near the fire and used for the men's afternoon sleep. The built-in beds occupied the warmest part of the house – by the chimney breast – and continued to be constructed until the end of the century in peasant homes; in Bavaria, they were decorated with flower painting.

RIGHT *The Winter Parlour from the castle of Wiggen in Switzerland. The room is furnished and panelled in pine, inlaid with other woods. The interior dates to 1582 and was completed to the order of Councillor Jacob Schlapprizi and his wife. It shows pine at its most spectacular.*

Pine beds in the Northern European style were especially popular with the followers of the various Arts & Crafts movements, who encouraged a new awareness and appreciation of folk art and furniture. In Sweden, the Society of Arts and Crafts was founded in 1845 in an attempt to combine artistic values and the new industrialization, which at the time was resulting in shoddy, mass-produced work. Schools of design and craft were set up in many parts of Germany in an attempt to foster traditional skills and help young workers to design progressive pieces that combined an honest use of natural materials with traditional forms.

This interest in folk styles has remained active in Germany and has recently become fashionable in other countries. Reproductions of four-poster, Gustavian and even Victorian styles are made in painted and waxed pine and can be used to create a special atmosphere in the bedroom. Spanish and Portuguese headboards with ornate carving and tall, turned pillars can look dramatic against plain walls, and a number of old patterns are now made in pine, which is sometimes gilded.

In general, antique American beds are much lighter in structure and have a closer resemblance to British rather than Northern European designs. Pine was often used in combination with other woods for turned beds, as beech and walnut were much more suitable for delicate but strong legs or bedposts. In the warmer parts of the country, heavy bed curtains were

BELOW *Renaissance-type decoration continued to be popular in Northern Sweden where fashions changed very slowly. This carved cradle dates to the 19th century and came from Overkalix in Norrbotten.*

LEFT *A Swedish Gustavian-type bed settee painted in red, a colour that was popular in Nederkalix in Norrbotten. The lower front section was pulled forward to form a bed.*

dispensed with, and a dainty lace canopy was often the only decoration for a four-poster with slender turning. German and Dutch craftsmen also produced furniture in the traditional styles of their countries of origin, and there are some splendid Norwegian rose-painted sleigh beds and four-posters.

Once mahogany bedroom furniture became necessary to indicate family affluence, pine declined in importance and was associated with secondary rooms and the homes of poorer people. The deal bedroom suites which could be purchased so cheaply in the late 19th century often included an almost surprisingly ornate bed constructed in imitation of the impressive mahogany designs. In cheaper beds, there was considerable use of slats for the headboards, the wide centre pieces being pierced or finished with machine carving. The original varnished finish makes some look unpleasantly cheap, but they come up well when stripped and waxed.

Comparatively few beds have survived, as they took up so much space and were discarded once they went out of fashion. The decorator can some-times locate an antique example, but these are quite expensive and it is often better to purchase a reproduction. Pine is now used to copy some of the designs that were originally intended for mahogany, with carved, somewhat rococo headboards which look impressive in French-style settings. Most craftsmen have a few designs that they will develop or adapt to individual specifications. Others create pine beds in a more artistic idiom, drawing on the better historical ideas to create country pieces that are not retrospective but, rather, modern work within the country tradition.

Cradles are among the items most frequently commissioned, as they can be carved with the infant's date of birth and initials and will become a family heirloom. Antique cradles have long attracted interior decorators, as they are small but very attractive objects that look good in many settings. They can be piled high with logs by a fireplace or used as a small blanket chest with the contents tied, German fashion, with coloured tapes or ribbons. They are ideal for use in the master bedroom during the baby's first months, especially if the effect of a room decorated with antiques would be spoiled by a modern carry cot.

The first cradles were hollowed-out sections of tree trunks, a method that is still used by some peoples. Another very simple design is a rectangular box-like structure with metal or wooden carrying handles at the sides. These were hung from the rafters in Northern European rooms and were sometimes painted. In Swedish country houses, there would be several hooks around the rooms so that the cradle could be hung in the most convenient position: near the parents' bed at night or in a cool breeze in the summer. Some of these were coloured red or green, others were left plain.

Large box-like cradles were used in the medieval period, but these were much more splendid and were hung between posts so they could be gently swung. The box part, which was deep, was piled high with mattresses so that the baby lay just below the top of the sides. This form was abandoned in the 18th century, when the box section was mounted on wooden rockers. This design has many regional variations and in north Sweden, for instance, the rockers are not across the head and foot of the cradle but run the length of the structure, so that the baby was rocked from head to foot rather than side to side. These long rockers were carved or painted, whereas the short rockers were left plain.

Most pine cradles have rocking posts at the corners to which the nurse could tie a scarf to make her job easier. In some prints and paintings, women are seen using these posts to help in the winding of wool. The cheapest cradles have plank sides, but better quality versions have small fielded panels or some carving or painting. There is often a hood to shelter the child's head from draughts; this also served to protect him from splashes when the cradle was used in the kitchen. In warmer countries, a headboard with carved or turned rails was more common, and cradles were shallower as the infant did not need as many blankets and mattresses. German cradles have small knobs along the sides for fastening the covers in place. When the cradle was not needed, the bedding was neatly folded and secured with ribbons.

Some cradles have hinged hoods to allow the baby to be lifted out more easily, while others have a compartment in the centre of the hood for the storage of spare clothes or a nursing apron. For very grand cradles, used for noble children, a pine construction was sometimes covered with velvet or brocade, although painted finishes were more common. Some pine was stained or grained to imitate other more expensive woods, especially mahogany, but these old finishes are rarely in good condition and are often stripped. Although most of the cradle designs date to the 17th and 18th centuries, these old styles continued in production until the Edwardian period, therefore construction methods and materials have to be used as a method of dating rather than the basic shapes.

BELOW A 19th-century German country bed with a tall headboard. It has applied turned decoration and was probably originally painted.

ABOVE Contrasting pine is used for added effect in this modern reconstruction of a 19th-century design.

Noble children were guarded with especial care once they were able to walk; instead of sleeping in low, adult-type beds, they were moved into a type of cupboard made from wooden slats, rather like a cage, where the child was always visible. These were mainly used in European countries but not, it seems, in Britain where children seem to have moved from the cradle into truckle-type beds.

Small children's beds were made in much greater variety in the United States, and both delicate four-posters dating from the 18th century and low 19th-century examples with turned posts and slatted or plank ends still exist. Proud parents could have the name of the child painted on the headboard, or the top rails flower-decorated by itinerant artists. Low children's beds seem to have been much more common in the United States than in Great Britain, where children who had grown too large for cots were moved, as they are today, into adult-length single beds.

Antique pine cradles and beds have always sold quickly, as they make fine christening gifts and are also valued by collectors of juvenilia. In the past, the cradle was moved from room to room as required, and it now looks appropriate in almost any part of the house. A few craftsmen make modern versions, although in general the selection is not very wide and there is room for more adventurous designs.

ABOVE Pine night stands are now used mainly as lamp tables and are here used in the gable bedroom of a hotel in Buckinghamshire, England.

ARCHITECTURAL PINE

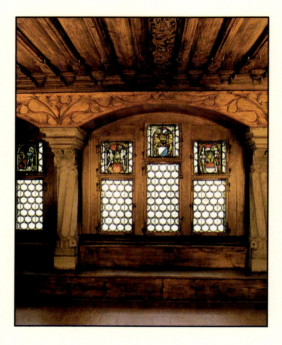

 WHEN INTERIOR DECORATORS NEEDED a section of panelling or a well-proportioned cupboard door, they used to seek the help of demolition companies, whose yards contained a random selection of bits and pieces from various buildings. Today, because of the interest in this area, there are many shops and warehouses specializing in the sale of window frames, pantry doors, fanlights and banister rails, so that almost any period effect can be created. Some firms offer dozens of pine doors, all stripped and waxed, in such a variety of quality and size that anything from a kitchen to a ballroom can be supplied.

Complete sections of panelling that once lined an 18th-century drawing room can, for instance, be found, together with the matching corner cupboards. With some adaptation, such fittings can transform a plain room, giving it an individuality that disappeared once household fittings became mass-produced. So great is the current demand for architectural pine antiques that reproductions are now manufactured, especially as the old sources of supply are fast dying out. Fortunately, conservation lobbies worldwide are now much more active, and old buildings are no longer sacrificed without very great consideration.

OPPOSITE *The Council Chamber from the Council House at Mellingen. Carved in the panelling is the inscription 'Uli Hans Widerker, Werchkmeister diser stat a.d. MCCCCLXVII/Der nit hat pfennig noch pfand der ess der truben ab der wand'. (Uli Hans Widerker, master craftsman of this town AD 1467 who has neither penny nor pledge and who eats the grapes off the wall.)*

ABOVE *The pine panelling, ceiling and furniture of the Council Chamber at Mellingen. The door case and door are made of oak.*

Many firms specializing in modern pine interiors provide Georgian and rococo panels, door cases and chimneypieces that can be made to fit rooms of almost any size. Elegant columns, cupboards and shelves, all in the same idiom, can be purchased to duplicate or maintain a particular period look. For anyone wishing to panel a complete hall or bathroom in pine, this is a much easier solution than attempting to find precisely the correct sizes in the stock of an antiques dealer. It is also inadvisable to cut down antique fittings as their value will be lowered; for difficult or small areas, such as a cloakroom, modern panelling is more sensible.

For decorative detail, dealers and auction houses are the obvious source of supply and can offer dressers, shelves and settles, all of which were originally built in to rooms. Georgian stripped-pine chimneypieces are now among the most desirable items, especially those with some additional detail such as a swag of carved ribbon and flowers. Originally, these chimneypieces were painted and sometimes gilded, but they are now preferred in their natural state. Large examples can be very expensive, but they are excellent investments, particularly since the character of a room is dominated by the style of the fireplace.

Much simpler pine surrounds, such as were used in many small town houses around 1900, also sell well and are used in combination with cast-iron grates and colourful tiles. Although these are still being removed from demolished houses, they are also reproduced and can be purchased quite cheaply since their construction is so simple. Any Victorian or Edwardian

LEFT *The Victorian hearth was the centre of domestic life but the fireplaces were ripped out of many houses in the 1950s and '60s. Today, replacements with waxed pine mantle* *surrounds are very popular and are even fitted in modern houses.*

ABOVE *An 18th-century pine mantle surround with Classical-style carved decoration. Such fine examples are now among the most sought after of all architectural pieces.*

chimneypiece with some additional ornament, such as a two-tier mantelshelf or brass inset panels, will attract interest, as do those with a matching over-mantel. Most of these fittings were originally stained in imitation of mahogany but now sell much more quickly when stripped. Occasionally, one of the plank chimneypieces once used in cottages comes on the market – this is ideal for a country retreat, with matching pine shelving built into the chimney alcoves on either side.

As pine was the cheapest wood, it was used for the complete range of household fittings, including settles, bookcases and beds. Such pieces are often difficult to remove without some damage, so a degree of restoration and replacement of parts has to be accepted. Most built-in furniture was made without backs, as it was supported by the walls: such pieces are now adapted into free-standing objects with the addition of boarding or panels. In some Georgian kitchens, the built-in dresser could occupy a complete wall, but these can look very ungainly when removed and converted.

Perhaps the most attractive of the architectural fittings are corner cupboards, with either a plain barrel or a carved shell-shaped top. Originally, many were fitted with panelled doors but these were frequently removed in the 1920s and 1930s, especially if the interior had shaped shelves for the display of china or glass. These corner cupboards vary in size, from delicate, elongated, single-door structures to towering and impressive pieces with double doors set between pillars. While a plain corner cupboard with a simple panelled door can be quite cheap, those with shell-carved tops and detailed cornices are classed among good antique furnishings and are correspondingly valued.

When the great 18th-century designers such as the Adam brothers designed library fittings to be painted and embellished with gilding, they chose pine for its low cost and the ease with which it could be worked. Some splendid classical-style bookcases with detailed cornices and pediments occasionally come on the market and are often stripped and polished before sale. These are among the most expensive of all pine furnishings, elegant and of such fine quality that they can show up other items in a room. As these bookcases were constructed for a wealthy and discerning market, their finish is superb; the shelves, though intended for books, are so nicely constructed that they are now frequently used for the display of collections of porcelain.

Oak and mahogany were fashionable woods for a library after 1800 but where the cost of these was too high, grained or stained pine was often used instead. Libraries in the Gothic taste, with arched or castellated tops to the cases, were thought appropriate for houses, churches and universities; a dark colour was required, however, in order to create a serious and worthy academic atmosphere. When stripped of several coats of paint, many of these library fittings take on a completely different character and become light and whimsical, more in the 18th-century Gothic idiom. The basic design of these bookcases, with adjustable slots or pegs to hold the shelves, is quite practical and it is hard to see why these structures cannot be copied by manufacturers of today, who tend to construct bookshelves for small volumes only.

OPPOSITE *In many Victorian and Edwardian houses original features have been removed. In this recently restored hall, replacement and original woodwork is well combined. The door and understairs panelling was originally dark painted or grained but is now stripped to give a lighter effect.*

Almost all old library shelves, and especially those with glass doors, are popular furnishings, as they provide excellent display space for collections. This need for display shelving has put a high premium on old shop fittings, and particularly those with ornate decoration such as spindle turnings. With their shallow, glass-fronted cabinets that were fitted floor-to-ceiling, chemists' shops evoke the atmosphere of a lost age; some of these fittings were stained and varnished to imitate mahogany and if in reasonable condition today should obviously be left or restored. When the surface is very distressed, there is sometimes little alternative to stripping, which has the advantage of achieving a much lighter effect.

Complete shop settings are costly, but can be seen in the stock of architectural warehouses and used with very little additional furniture for a

BELOW *By stripping this wide window frame, a country look is given to a modern kitchen with tiled walls which would have seemed cold without the warmth of the wood.*

dining room. If they are integrated without too much adaptation, they form an excellent investment, as the number of period shops being demolished is happily decreasing each year.

In comparison, church and chapel fittings still appear regularly on the market and are often surprisingly cheap, considering the quality of the workmanship. Sections of rail and gallery, a complete pulpit, steps and screens all offer numerous decorating possibilities. Much of this furniture was stained and grained and benefits from stripping. As it is not as yet in short supply, adaptation and conversion do not seem too much of a crime, so sections of a screen could be used for a bed-head or an old notice board can be used for telephone messages in the hall or kitchen.

As municipal buildings are improved and refurbished, similar fittings to those in chapels appear in the stock of demolition companies. They can sometimes supply such items as pine arches, a panelled door or a section of rail in high Gothic style, all pieces that can be used to make a modern or early 20th-century house more interesting. Often, just one section from a 19th-century building can establish a theme of decoration – whether in solid Victorian style or light-hearted Chinoiserie – that can be augmented with secondary modern fittings.

ABOVE *Old shop fittings are now in great demand for domestic use. These drawers, from a drapers or ironmongers, make an excellent kitchen dresser base.*

BUYING
AND
LOOKING AFTER
PINE

WHEN PINE FURNITURE IS DESIRED for its effect in a particular setting rather than as an investment, then it is cheaper to buy reproductions or modern work. There are pine suppliers in most towns where kitchen units, refectory tables and chests of drawers can be selected from large stocks. Individual craftsmen can be commissioned to equip a room of difficult or small proportions, so that a pleasing overall look can be achieved. The cost of having furniture custom-made can be surprisingly low when compared to mass-produced pieces, and there is the extra satisfaction that comes from designing a complete room and supervising every detail of its construction. As fashion and taste are now so relaxed, the decorator can select from any styles of the past or can mix some of the most successful ideas, to create a completely individual arrangement.

LEFT *Genuine pieces of old pine are sometimes painted. This chest, with attractive arched panels, has been decorated by Dragons of Walton Street, London, who create decoration in any style.*

OPPOSITE *A dresser in the restoration workshop of a Welsh pine dealer. As pine is a soft wood, susceptable to damage, sections frequently have to be replaced.*

When commissioning a craftsman, it is necessary to see several examples of his work rather than rely on photographs, which can be very misleading. Examine the prestige and run-of-the-mill pieces for finish, proportion and good, basic joinery; look in cupboards and under drawers, making sure that the timber used for each section is appropriate, as some try to cut costs by using wood that should have been discarded. If the general quality and design of the work are satisfactory, then talk to the craftsman about your requirements. Most woodworkers enjoy talking about their work and the way they have solved various design problems for other customers and will see it as part of their function as craftsmen to encourage your participation.

When expensive furniture or fittings are commissioned, ask to see the working drawings and confirm that each stage meets with your satisfaction. It is unfair to allow a joiner to complete a bed-head in Renaissance style before he is told that rustic Spanish would have been preferred. Some craftsmen specialize in a limited number of designs which they have found to be popular and can be made up in any size. In this case, no stage participation is necessary, as finished examples will have been seen in the showroom. But check that the finish of the piece is as good as that of the display model: some firms are so busy that work is contracted out and unless very strict quality control is maintained, people can be disappointed.

The finest craftsman-made modern pine can prove to be a good investment if it is purchased from a well-known maker whose products are marked or identifiable by some special device or motif. Look out for woodworkers whose work is exhibited at important events or has been purchased by museums or galleries, as the products of a known maker are more likely to be of interest in the future. There are an ever-increasing number of craftsmen who are reintroducing traditional methods of making and finishing, but they do need support in order to maintain their operations.

The best guide to the age of pine is the overall wear and patination of the wood. Makers of reproductions now use an antique varnish which gives an overall brown tint, but genuine patination is much softer and varies in different parts of the structure. Those sections that are always exposed to light, such as the fronts of cupboards and tops of tables, have invariably changed colour, while the backs and sides of drawers will have altered much less. As softwoods mark easily, be suspicious of a piece with no scars or signs of wear, especially on plinths or the edges of chests of drawers or coffers. Kitchen tables were particularly prone to staining and damage, so an example with a pristine finish is either a replacement or has been planed down. Replaced tops do not cause much concern on tables made after 1850 as they are still relatively cheap; but a Regency or 18th-century table should be examined with care, as a new top would considerably affect its value.

If the finish of some section of a dresser, for instance, is much smoother than the rest of the piece, then begin to search for more evidence of restoration. Check that the method of dovetailing is identical on all the drawers and that the wood used on all the drawer sides is the same. Examine the back and the sides to confirm that there are no new parts. As pine continues to shrink over a long period, this can always be seen, especially in panelled furniture. Originally, most panels were set into grooves to allow them to expand and contract naturally, so a number should feel a little loose. Panels that are fixed rigidly in position cause more concern, as replacements are sometimes glued or even nailed.

Many of the problems connected with genuine antique pine stem from the practice of repairing damaged furniture by nailing. As country furniture of this kind was cheap, it was rarely professionally restored and the loose arms of settles, the bottoms of drawers and even loose panels were roughly fixed back in position, a practice that has led to bad splits and chips.

As drawers shrink less than the framework of a chest, they are often the cause of loose back-boards. On fine furniture there were stops that could be adjusted as the drawers moved out of position, but this was rarely done on pine and the constant use will have resulted in a loosening of the back panels

ABOVE *Simple side tables, bought in a distressed condition, can be stripped and polished to provide useful pieces of furniture.*

LEFT *The fashion for antique pine has fostered many imaginative re-creations. Here a Victorian washstand design has been adapted to provide a handbasin for a bathroom or cloakroom.*

– not a cause for concern, however. The runners of the old drawers should be very smooth because of wear: if they seem rough, then look at the piece with care, although it should be remembered that if it has been recently stripped, the process will have opened up the grain and caused roughness, which can be sanded down again.

On furniture such as settles with turned legs and arms be suspicious about crisply even arm supports. Because of natural aging and wear, they should no longer be mathematically even but have moved just a little off true. Other indications are fairly obvious, such as new handles or hinges or a lock without a lock plate above, suggesting that the drawer is a replacement. As the screws and nails on pine have often been replaced, they can only provide a general guide to the originality of the piece. When they appear to be old, they can provide helpful clues as to the date of construction. Rectangular nails, stamped from a sheet and with flat sides, were still used in country areas until the late 18th century and can be recognized without difficulty. Early nails also have uneven heads, as machine-made versions did not come into general use until around 1815. The presence of such nails is not a positive indication of age, since they can be reused by the makers of fake furniture. Fortunately, the price of pine is not yet high enough to attract highly skilled fakers.

The type of nails employed today, wire nails, have sharp round points and came into general use after 1850; their heads invariably show discolouration if they have been in place for some time. As nails often work loose, re-nailed parts are common, but look for the original nail holes alongside. Metal screws might also seem to be a recent development, but they have been used on furniture from around 1700; very early versions can be identified by their narrow slots, which are not always centrally positioned. As metal screws were expensive, they were rarely used on country furniture before 1830. After this date, many improvements and inventions resulted in the pointed screw, which is found on most Victorian furniture. Like nails, screws were frequently replaced, but the presence of some originals is always encouraging.

Some early pine was peg-jointed with sections of wood that were kiln-dried, inserted in the joint, and allowed to expand with the natural moisture of the atmosphere to create a firm structure. Sometimes, the original pegs will have fallen out and a modern dowel (which is mechanically turned) will have been used instead. This type of dowel came into use around 1850. Before that time, pegs used for this type of work were slightly uneven.

All these elements – nails, screws, patination and replacement parts – can only be taken individually as a general indication that there might be something wrong with the piece. This should set mental warning bells ringing and if more disquieting elements are found, then leave well alone.

Personal judgements are especially important when buying at auction, where the catalogue descriptions are written with the protection of disclaimers. Efforts are being made to bring the conditions under which goods are sold at auction more in line with those under which shopkeepers operate; in several countries, however, such transactions are still a somewhat grey

ABOVE *Pedestal stands provide useful storage for small items. They are now frequently used for the display of pieces of sculpture. Examples can be found in most good antique shops.*

LEFT *A good pine cricket table with an unfortunate plastic top for sale in a Cardiff auction room. Such pieces can be purchased relatively cheaply because of the necessity for careful restoration.*

BELOW *A good variety of furniture accessories in traditional designs can now be located. In this instance replacement china knobs have been used on an old chest of drawers.*

area of the law. The general advice when purchasing any type of antique furniture is: buy what you like, what you believe to be authentic, and at a price you feel is supportable. Then accept a good return on a well-considered investment or a small loss on a piece that should have been bought with more care. This is the attitude taken by most antiques dealers who, after years of buying and selling, still make the occasional mistake. Happily, as you become more experienced in examining furniture, you will develop an eye for a correct piece – a much better guide than a minute examination of the structure.

Concern for antique furniture does not end at the point of purchase, for its value is best protected by careful use and regular cleaning. All pine furniture, antique or modern, is preferably kept in a cool atmosphere with slight humidity. The temperature should ideally be constant, as in good museums, and no sunlight should fall on the surfaces. Obviously, such conditions are impractical in most homes, although a few basic precautions can be taken to protect the more valuable pieces.

TOP *Painted pine is currently fashionable and gives an American country atmosphere to this modern kitchen.*

ABOVE *Sections of panelling, doors and chests awaiting purchase in a pine sellers yard.*

Painted antique pine is most at danger, as the surface is easily chipped and the paint will bubble or lift if anything very hot touches it. It is very important to keep such items out of the sun as the colours might fade, although muslin curtains will help to filter the damaging ultraviolet rays. The furniture should be dusted regularly with a very soft cotton cloth and waxed with a polish obtained from a specialist in restoration materials once or twice a year. Modern polishes are not suitable for old, painted furnishings and it is best to use a traditional substance that has been well tested.

Plain pine should be kept free from dust and should be waxed and polished regularly to maintain and improve the surface. If the wood has been stripped, it will need years of waxing and buffing before a satisfactory surface is achieved. If a chest of drawers has brass handles that need cleaning, remember to protect the surrounding softwood, as it will mark easily. Servants used to have cardboard templates to protect furniture and paint-work when they were cleaning the brass; that method is still occasionally used for pieces frequently at risk.

If a pine table is used in the dining room or kitchen, be careful to mop up any spills immediately or the softwood will be stained. If any stain has sunk into the wood, then consult a hardware shop specializing in restoration materials; they will suggest a suitable paste or bleach.

When moving heavy pine furniture, it is best to take out parts such as drawers and shelves to avoid putting too much strain on the frame. If it has to be transported, it should be protected by at least one thick blanket, otherwise the surface could be bruised or scratched. Even rough pine purchased for restoration should be protected in this way, as a blanket tied firmly around the item will help to contain any loose pieces that might break off in transit.

The best restoration can result in furniture looking untouched and completely original. To this end, as little work as possible should be undertaken and no 'improvements' should be added. If the piece is very dirty, then brush and dust it thoroughly to remove any grime from ledges, mouldings and handles.

Avoid washing, as detergents will damage any patina and hot water will loosen old glue. Instead, use a white spirit and linseed oil mixture or a brand-name cleaner based on alcohol and turpentine which will remove accumulated dirt and wax. The container will have full instructions, but be careful not to overclean old furniture as it should not look new.

A high quality wax polish should then be applied. For an especially fine polish the wax may be applied with the finest grade steel wool before a final polishing with a soft cloth.

If complete restoration is needed and old paint has to be stripped, then first remove all fittings such as knobs and key plates, retaining any original screws so they can be replaced. If these metal parts are dirty, they can be cleaned in a small basin of commercial stripper before they are rinsed and polished.

BELOW A good pine dresser that was originally a fitting in an 18th-century kitchen. When restored this will be a very attractive piece despite its large size.

LEFT The interior of an antique shop that specializes in antique pine furniture.

To strip the piece, it can be sent to a professional who will clean the surface by immersion in a tank of caustic soda. Tank stripping can leave an unpleasant crystalline pink or white residue, and if the furniture was made before 1850, it would be preferable to clean the surface by scraping. Old dealers often used a piece of broken bottle glass for this purpose, as it was not as likely to scar the surface as a knife. This method of hand stripping is very slow but has the great advantage of keeping the wood in a natural state and not removing the natural oils.

If a chemical stripper is used, then follow the maker's instructions with care and, if possible, work out of doors. Most liquid strippers are brushed onto the paint and allowed to soak in before the loosened surface is scraped off. Usually several coats are needed before the wood is clean and this, inevitably, softens the surface of the wood, making it so fragile that it can be marked badly if the stripping tool is used carelessly. Recently, peel-off strippers have become more popular: they are intended to remove all the layers in one operation.

While most strippers can be washed off the furniture, caustic soda has to be hosed off in a well-drained yard and then allowed to dry out naturally. When completely dry, the wood should be sanded with the grain, starting with a coarse grade and then finishing with a fine glass paper. If there are any holes or cracks, these can be stopped with a tinted filler, although longer cracks sometimes need a sliver of matching wood that has to be glued in place. If any of the joints are loose, these have to be taken apart, cleaned and reglued with a woodworking adhesive before the complete piece is again sanded. Modern pine is sometimes varnished with tinted polyurethane, but this should not be used on any pre-1940 pieces as it creates a completely wrong surface effect; the restorer's aim, at all times, is to make the furniture regain its original appearance. If, because of immersion in a stripping tank, an old piece looks too scrubbed and fresh then a light tinted stain might be required, but try it out on a hidden part before it is applied to the complete piece, as colour charts often have little relationship to the tint on very soft woods.

In any of this work, the amateur can be helped by several books on the subject, and restoration courses and classes are held in many towns and education centres. If a professional restoration is decided upon, then be sure to specify the extent of your requirements. It is often easier to replace a complete section rather than work on small insertions in carefully matched woods, so that the degree of work undertaken in the name of 'restoration' is often alarming. In order to protect antique furniture from such attacks, specify in detail exactly what you require and make sure that no heavy varnish is applied to help conceal poor work.

With sensible daily care, pine furniture will repay the time and concern expended on its restoration by giving years of satisfaction to the user. Unlike mass-produced furniture, it will never fall in value, while its interest and history will continue to attract interior decorators, especially those working in the country idiom.

TOP Restored furniture and pieces still in an unrenovated, rough state are sold in most auction rooms, where the majority of dealers obtain their stock.

ABOVE Many market stands now specialize in pine furniture. This corner of the Great Western Antiques Centre in Bath, England, gives some conception of the variety that is offered to the home decorator.

GLOSSARY

▍BALUSTER Post or pillar with turned decoration, usually bulbous.

▍BAROQUE Richly ornamented with flowing curves.

▍BIEDERMEIER German style of the period 1815–1848.

▍BEST KITCHEN The Dutch housewife displayed her finest possessions in the Best kitchen; another room was used for the rougher work.

▍CANTED CORNERS Obliquely faced.

▍CELURE The section of a bed below the tester.

▍CUT WORK BACKS Open work cutting.

▍DENTILLED EDGE Square toothed form, usually made from small rectangular blocks.

▍DOWEL TURNING Lathe-turned wood of equal circular section.

▍FEDERAL STYLE American 1790–1850.

▍FIELDED PANELS Panels with shaped edges.

▍FRET-CUTTING Geometrical ornament, sometimes in openwork.

▍FRIEZE A band of pattern on a flat surface.

▍GIRANDOLE 18th-century form of mirror-backed candle sconce.

▍'H' HINGES Hinges in the shape of the letter 'H'.

▍INCISING Decoration that is gouged or scraped out.

▍JAPANNED Imitation lacquer.

▍LOW BACK RACKS A low shelf area at the back.

▍MORTISE AND TENNON JOINT Formed with a projecting tongue that fits into a rectangular slot.

▍MOULDED CORNICE Top edging decorated with moulding.

▍MULE CHEST A coffer with drawers at the foot.

▍PEDIMENT A gable-shaped top, originally seen on Classical temples.

▍PIER TABLES Designed to stand against a pier – e.g. between windows.

▍PLANK CONSTRUCTION Simple furniture, made from joined planks.

▍ROCOCO Decorative style, based on rock and shell forms.

▍SLEIGH BED A north European bed in the form of a sleigh.

▍SPLAT The central vertical between the seat and the top rail of a chair.

▍STEPPED BASE A base in the form of inverted steps.

▍STILES Vertical part of framework.

▍STRETCHERS Horizontals that link the legs and strengthen the construction.

▍TENTER FRAME Framework of a canopied bed.

▍TESTER The canopy section of a bed.

▍TURNED Wood shaped on a lathe.

INDEX

Page numbers in *italics* refer to captions.

CREDITS

Key: *l* = left; *r* = right; *t* = top; *b* = bottom.

THE AMERICAN MUSEUM IN BRITAIN, BATH/PHOTOS. DEREK BALMER: pages 11, 20 *t b*, 28/29, 54 *l*, 75, 96, 98/99. HARRIET ANN SLEIGH BEDS: page 100. AUTHOR: pages 8 *t*, 9, 16, *tl bl*, 33, 35, 59 *r*. THE BRIDGEMAN ART LIBRARY: pages 6 (Victoria & Albert Museum, London); 17 (Dark & Rendlesham, London; 64 (Read and Partners, Crewe); 77 (Bibi Harris Ltd). THE CHEQUERS INN, BUCKINGHAMSHIRE: pages 32, 107. CHRISTIES, NEW YORK: page 50. COLONIAL WILLIAMSBURG FOUNDATION: pages 7, 30, 63, 68, *l*, 78 *b*. DRAGONS OF WALTON STREET, LONDON: page 117. LIZ EDDISON: page 87. EVODE: page 89. JAYCEE FURNITURE: pages 13, 67, 92, 101. JOHN LEWIS OF HUNGERFORD: pages 48, 58/59, 61, 68 *r*. MANOR BARN PINE: page 71 *t*. NATIONAL MUSEUM OF FINLAND: pages 14/15, 22, 24, 40/41, 42, 44, 45, 47, 54 *r*, 62, 69, 70, 72 *l r*, 78 *t*, 97. THE NATIONAL TRUST PHOTOGRAPHIC LIBRARY: pages 38, 51, 52/3, 55, 56, 76. PETER NEWARK'S WESTERN AMERICANA: page 18/19. NORDISKA MUSEET, STOCKHOLM: pages 8 *b*, 16 *tr*, 23, 25, 39 *l r*, 57, 65, 66, 71 *b*, 88, 104, 105. PIPE DREAMS: page 118/119. QUARTO PUBLISHING PLC/PHOTOS. MICHAEL MICHAELS: pages 80, 90, 112/113, 114. REAL FLAME: page 110/111. SMALLBONE KITCHENS: page 21. SOTHEBY'S, NEW YORK: pages 19, 26, 27. STIRLING RONCRAFT: pages 34, 119 *r*, 122 *t*. JESSICA STRANG: pages 60 *r*, 79, 81, 82/83, 91 *r*, 115. SWISS NATIONAL MUSEUM, ZURICH: pages 31, 102/103, 108, 109. TOP KNOBS: page 121 *b*. ULSTER FOLK AND TRANSPORT MUSEUM: pages 36, 37. JANE VANDELL ASSOCIATES: pages 10, 85 *l r*, 86, 94, 111 *r*, 120 (Cleveland Antiques and Fine Art, Ross-on-Wye); 12 (Diana Moss, Paragon Antiques Market, Bath); 49, 93, 116, 122 *b*, (Mary Booth Antiques, Swansea); 60 *l*, 121 *t*, 123 *t*, 124 *t* (Phillips, Cardiff); 74, 106 *t b*, 123 *b* (The Old Pine Shop, Ross-on-Wye); 84 (Graham Corke, Bath); 95 (Crofton Antiques, Bath); 124 *b* (Great Western Antiques Centre, Bath).